MW00938557

# Penny Stocks Mastery

*Complete Beginner's Guide to Building Riches Through the Stock Market*

**James Hawk**

*James Hawk*

# © Copyright 2016 - All rights reserved.

In no way is it legal to reproduce, duplicate, or transmit any part of this document in either electronic means or in printed format. Recording of this publication is strictly prohibited and any storage of this document is not allowed unless with written permission from the publisher. All rights reserved.

The information provided herein is stated to be truthful and consistent, in that any liability, in terms of inattention or otherwise, by any usage or abuse of any policies, processes, or directions contained within is the solitary and utter responsibility of the recipient reader. Under no circumstances will any legal responsibility or blame be held against the publisher for any reparation, damages, or monetary loss due to the information herein, either directly or indirectly. Respective authors own all copyrights not held by the publisher.

Legal Notice:

This book is copyright protected. This is only for personal use. You cannot amend, distribute, sell, use, quote or paraphrase any part or the content within this book without the consent of the author or copyright owner. Legal action will be pursued if this is breached.

Disclaimer Notice:

Please note the information contained within this document is for educational and entertainment purposes only. Every attempt has been made to provide accurate, up to date and reliable complete information. No warranties of any kind are expressed or implied. Readers acknowledge that the author is not engaging in the rendering of legal, financial, medical or professional advice.

By reading this document, the reader agrees that under no circumstances are we responsible for any losses, direct or indirect, which are incurred as a result of the use of information contained within this document, including, but not limited to — errors, omissions, or inaccuracies.

# Table of Contents

*James Hawk*

# Introduction

The stock market is a vast place where thousands of transactions take place every day, all over the world. Most of us have a vague idea of what it is and how it works, but few people really understand it and how to work with it. This book is aimed to help you become one of those few people.

Stock markets are physical places where buyers and sellers converge daily to buy and sell stocks and other financial securities in order to capitalize upon their ever-changing values. There are many types of financial securities that people can invest in, with the most preferred ones being stocks.

Stocks or shares are part of a company, which are issued to the public on a regular basis. There are many types of stocks such as ordinary, preferred, and penny stocks. In this book, we will look at the last type in detail to understand what penny stocks stand for.

This book is a complete and thorough guide to penny stocks and penny stock trading. While penny stock trading can be complicated, as can any type of stock trading, this book will provide you with the information necessary for you to understand penny stock trading and will leave you ready to start trading in penny stocks once you have completed the entire book.

We will take you from the basics of defining penny stocks and associated concepts so that you understand the basic terminology and concepts of penny stock trading before getting more in depth into the topic.

Then we will move into how to get started in penny stock trading, where you will be given information about the basic resources that you need to be properly prepared to trade in penny stocks.

After that, we will discuss how the prices of penny stocks are calculated. Valuation and share price are complicated concepts, with a variety of factors that come into play, and this book will take you through those various factors and explain how each impacts the price of a penny stock.

Once you understand the basics of penny stock pricing, we will move into how to select the penny stocks in which you are going to invest. This section will look at factors to consider when choosing both the company and the specific stocks in which you will be investing. There are several criteria to consider when determining whether a penny stock is the right investment opportunity for you.

The next chapter goes through an extensive and in-depth examination of the various ways in which the price of penny stocks can be predicted. There are a number of methods and they can seem quite complicated. However, after reading through this section you will have a clear understanding of the different methods, the data that they provide, and how you can use them to make your investment decisions.

Next, we will look at the analysis methods for penny stocks. This includes analysis of a company's fundamentals, such as the income statement, balance sheet, and cash flow statement. It also includes an alternative analysis method, the technical analysis, which examines a company's share price patterns and trends. All of these analysis techniques are useful and they should be used in conjunction with each other when determining which penny stocks you are interested in purchasing.

Then we will look at day trading, what it is, and why you should day-trade in penny stocks. While some people may think that day trading is not appropriate for penny stocks, this section will explain that it certainly can be appropriate, and why it might be the right decision for you.

After this is an examination of the dos and don'ts of penny stocks: What you absolutely should do and what you should avoid if you are going to start trading in penny stocks. Dos include creating an investment plan and making investment rules for yourself, while don'ts include getting caught up in investment schemes and expecting to become rich overnight. This section has a lot of general but practical information that will help you to successfully invest in penny stocks.

We will then move into myths and FAQs of penny stocks and clear up some common misunderstandings that you may also have about penny stocks and penny stock trading. We will also review the advantages and disadvantages of penny stocks so that you have a clear idea of what you can and cannot expect from trading in penny stocks.

The next chapter will go through some important terminologies that you will need to know and understand in order to successfully navigate the world of penny stocks. These terminologies are applicable not only to penny stock trading but to trading in higher-value stocks, as well.

Then we will discuss the different types of trade exchanges, market traders, and market indices, which will give you a clear understanding of the trading system and how to operate within it. After that, we will look at the various kinds of brokers and promoters you might encounter during your ventures into the world of penny stock trading, and will discuss which of these can be helpful to you and which are best avoided.

Finally, we will end with the most important rules to follow when investing in penny stocks, including carrying out comprehensive and proper research and implementing damage control as soon as possible if you discover that you have made a bad decision. These rules, if you follow them, will play a significant role in allowing you to earn profits and avoid losses. The last section of the book is a summary of the key highlights of the book and is a useful section to return to remind yourself of essential concepts and ideas about penny stock trading.

Many people view penny stocks are a very risky investment. You may have heard people say that trading in the stock market is like gambling. For the uninformed investor, this may be the case, but if you do your homework, inform yourself, and understand how the market works, penny stock trading can become a very lucrative hobby or means of building capital. Reading this book will help calm your nerves and let you understand better how to invest money without experiencing what we all fear - losing it all.

Once you have read all of the sections and are sure that you understand the information provided, you will be fully prepared to enter the world of penny stock trading and start making your investment decisions. Then the next step will be up to you. Which penny stocks will you choose? There is only one way to find out: read this book, and then get started on investing!

Let us begin.

*James Hawk*

# Chapter 1

# What Are Penny Stocks?

First and foremost, I wish to thank you for choosing this book and hope you have a good time reading it. We will be explaining all the aspects of penny stock trading in detail, so you don't need to have any prior experience. Consider this book your all-in-one guide for a new venture in your life.

In this first chapter of the book, we will look at what penny stocks stand for and what you should know about them in order to invest in them.

Penny stocks are those that are priced at $5 and under. However, just because they are called penny stocks does not mean they will only cost a penny, just as many items you find at a Dollar Store are more expensive than a dollar.

Although they could cost just a penny, not many stocks these days are priced that low and so you will rarely find something that cheap in the market. The name was originally given over a hundred years ago, back when penny stocks actually went for a penny. However, these days, the price of penny stocks usually ranges between $1 and $5.

Another criterion of penny stocks, according to the Securities & Exchange Commission (SEC), is that they are not listed on the national exchange. Often other criteria are added as well, but these change frequently. To stay up to date, it is best to consult the current SEC guidelines.

There are various definitions of penny stocks, depending on who you ask in the industry. The SEC defines a penny stock as any stock priced under $5. Others set the definition as under $3, and some even will only consider a stock a penny stock if it's priced under $1. Still others will consider a stock to be a penny stock if it is traded on the pink sheets, which are daily lists put together by the National Quotation Bureau. Companies with stocks listed on the pink sheets (i.e., not on the stock exchange) do not need to meet certain minimum requirements and do not have to file with the SEC. In other countries, such as Great

Britain, penny stocks are referred to as cent stocks and may have different criteria. In England, for example, a cent stock must be under £1 rather than $1. If you wish to trade internationally, you will want to familiarize yourself with the standards set in each country.

The term "penny stocks" is generally used interchangeably with the term "micro-cap stocks," although there is a minor difference between the two. Penny stocks, as mentioned above, are classified based on the price that you would pay to purchase the stocks, whereas micro-cap stocks are identified by their market capitalization.

Market capitalization is the total dollar market value of all of the shares of a company and is calculated by multiplying the current market price of one of the company's shares by the number of the company's shares that are outstanding. Typically, a stock that has a market capitalization between $50 million and $300 million will be classified as a micro-cap stock.

Nanocap stocks also fall into the category of penny stocks. Nanocap stocks are microcap stocks that have a market capitalization of less than $50 million. The trick with these types of stocks is that it is very hard to get information about them from the general trading community. Trades are most often done by insiders who have information about the company in question and its products that is not generally available to the public. For this reason, it is often harder to get in on these trades, unless you know more about the company personally.

If you have watched "Wolf of Wall Street," you will have a rough idea of what penny stocks are. You will also know that Jordan Belfort made millions by trading in them.

However, it might not be possible for everyone to make millions out of penny stocks, as they can be tricky to understand and their trends tough to predict. There are four main factors that make penny stocks more of a risk than blue chip stocks: 1) lack of information; 2) no minimum standards; 3) lack of history; and 4) low liquidity.

The first factor, lack of information, is with respect to investment information that is made available to the public. For penny stocks and micro-cap stocks, the information is much harder to find because many of the companies are not required to file with the SEC. This also means that the information that is available is not always as reliable and credible as information that is made available for stocks that are listed on the NYSE and NASDAQ, for example.

As mentioned above, stocks that are listed on pink sheets do not have to meet the same minimum standard requirements as other stocks do that are listed on an exchange. The minimum standards are seen by many investors as a benchmark by which they measure the viability of stocks. Companies listed on the pink sheets often include companies that were no longer able to maintain their status on a major exchange, and therefore moved to the pink sheets so that the same filing requirements would not be applicable. These companies, also known as "fallen angels," would be a significant risk for an investor.

This removal of minimum standards of reporting leads to the third risk factor, which is a lack of history. Many of the companies that will be considered penny stocks are either new and just starting to build their financial strength, or they are on a downswing in terms of financial health as mentioned above. Companies such as these will likely have little to no track record that is available to potential investors, which can make it difficult to determine the potential of that company's stock.

Finally, penny stocks tend to have low liquidity, which causes two problems: difficulty selling the stock and easily manipulated stock prices. A low liquidity can make a penny stock less appealing to a potential buyer, so you may have difficulty selling when the time comes. This may result in your having to lower the price sufficiently to interest a buyer. As for manipulated stock prices, this can be done in several ways, but the most common is for an investor to purchase large quantities of the stock, promote the stock extensively, and then sell it once the investor has made it attractive enough to buyers. This is known in the trading industry as the "pump and dump."

This is not at all to say that penny stocks are not worth learning about or investing in. If done properly, penny stocks can make for lucrative investments, provided you know which ones to pick and how long to hold. In time, you will understand how it really works and what you should do to capitalize on their fluctuating prices. This book will provide you with a thorough guide to navigating the world of penny stocks. After reading this book, you will be equipped with the necessary knowledge to make an educated and informed decision about whether you want to invest in penny stocks and which penny stocks to choose if you do decide to invest.

Penny stocks have existed for quite some time now. They are traded mostly in the day markets, as their prices keep moving up and down, making them ideal for scalpers. Think of a scalper as a bargain shopper who resells his product. Scalpers find stocks that are being offered at below market value, and they know they have customers who are willing to pay that market price. They purchase the stocks at a "bargain," and then turn around and sell them at full price. This means they have a guaranteed profit, regardless of whether the stock price goes up or not, as long as they are able to sell at market value. This is a completely legitimate and legal form of trade, and shouldn't be confused with fraudulent scalping, which involves manipulating the market.

Penny stocks are preferred to regular stocks because of their low prices. If you have a budget of just $100 a day, you can buy several penny stocks from different categories.

Penny stocks are mostly bought by old hands, who have relevant experience in stock market trading. But that does not mean newbies cannot trade in them. It is all about knowing where and when to invest.

Penny stocks are generally not traded on major stock exchanges such as New York Stock Exchange owing to their volatility and low prices. They are traded over the counter through the issuance of pink sheets. These sheets are meant to represent the value of money that the person is willing to invest in them. This trend in OTC stocks is now gaining widespread popularity because of the ease of use. You need not shell out money every time that you wish to buy stocks and can settle for certificates that give you the stocks in return.

One major point to note about penny stocks is their volatile nature. These stocks can rise and fall in value within a short period of time and it is important for people to understand how a particular stock's graph will move. Due to the low value of penny stocks, they can double or drop to half very quickly. For example, if you invested in a penny stock that is 10 cents per share, and it drops 2 cents, you have already lost 20% of your investment. On the other hand, if it goes up 2 cents, you have made a 20% profit in an incredibly short amount of time.

This volatility can be attributed to a lot of different reasons. It might come about owing to majority investors trying to control the market by pumping and dumping stocks. It might also be because of volatile market conditions where the demand might not match the supply or vice versa. So it is quite difficult to pinpoint something in particular and it would be beneficial if the investor understood all the different elements involved in detail.

Penny stocks are also known for their high pay-off rate. It is quite possible for you to turn a small investment into a big one just by choosing the right stocks to invest in. It would not be an exaggeration to say that penny stocks can bring in millions through just a small investment.

However, there is a catch in it. Before you start investing in penny stocks, you have to know that not a lot of information will be available about the stocks of your choice. You will have to dig deep to find information about them without which, you might run the risk of losing out on your investment. Many brokers refuse to invest in penny stocks as they assume the worst, so your broker might not jump at the prospect of helping you acquire penny stocks and will advise you to exercise caution.

There will always be a looming risk of liquidity with penny stocks. Penny stocks are not quite popular on a large enough scale to make investing in them equivalent to investing in the stock of a lesser-known company. Not many investors will be aware of their existence and that will play a big part in reducing the salability of these stocks.

The demand and supply theory for these stocks works just as it does for any regular stocks. If there is great demand for a stock, its price will rise and, if demand is low, its price will fall. This is a universal concept and will affect penny stock prices the same as with regular stocks.

If you are keen on investing in them, you must understand every single aspect in order to ensure that you safeguard your money. You must not go into something without accounting for its downside. If you have a doubt about something, you must immediately seek information on it and make sure that your doubt is fully cleared.

If you want to be as thorough as possible when you are deciding which penny stocks to purchase, gather a list of all of the penny stocks that are available, start to whittle the list down by looking at various factors. First, take out any penny stocks that do not generate revenue. Then remove any from the list that do not have operational websites that include contact information for and details about the company. If the company is not making it easy to obtain information about it, consider this a red flag. Once you have narrowed down the list that far, look for companies that offer liquid stock, are debt-free or at least offer a strong balance sheet, and are either reducing their losses or, preferably, making a profit. You might also consider looking into the executives of the company to see their past histories. A CEO who has bankrupted several companies before the current one is probably not one you want to rely on to ensure that the current company will be profitable.

When you go through these factors, it will remove the vast majority of penny stocks from your list. Then, you will be left with a list of investments that are most likely to be safe, reliable, and profitable.

Through the course of this book, we will look at the different aspects of penny stocks in detail to ensure that you get a full view. You will have to spend some time thinking about your decision to invest in them and ensure that you are thoroughly satisfied with your final choice.

# Chapter 2

# Basic Penny Stock Concepts

Hopefully you now have a good idea of what penny stocks are. There are still a few more aspects of penny stocks that you should understand before jumping head-first into the fray. In this chapter, we are going to outline some basic penny stock concepts that you must understand in order to trade in them effectively.

## Stocks

This one might seem a little easy, but it is important to understand exactly what it is that you will be investing in. A stock is basically a piece of paper (whether literal or metaphorical) that entitles you to a percentage of ownership in a company. That piece of paper is assigned a value, based on multiple factors, which is called the share price.

Some form of stock has been in existence since the Roman Empire and it has evolved into what we now know as shares of a company. A company's value is calculated on its current equity or worth if the company were to be dissolved and all its assets sold. That amount is then divided by the number of shares that the company has released, which gives you the price of one stock. A company can at any time increase the number of shares it offers. Rapidly growing companies will do this frequently, and this is often a sure sign of growth and profit opportunity. To understand the total worth of a company, simply multiply the stock price by its number of shares.

Stocks are also not a purely Western invention. Other countries such as Nigeria and Saudi Arabia also have exchanges. However, the majority of trading in the world is done in North America, Europe, and Asia, which combined trade over 80% of the world's stocks. Starting out, you will want to stick to the exchange in your home country, but trading internationally can be just as rewarding and interesting. Just make sure you educate yourself before you undertake such an endeavor.

## Portfolio

The portfolio includes all the stocks that you hold at any given point in time. Your portfolio is the sum total of all financial securities that you hold and will give you a clear picture of the type of investments that you have made. A portfolio includes not only your stocks, but also any precious metal investments, the worth of any IRAs, and any other investments, regardless of type.

Everybody's portfolio looks different and it is a matter of personal choice. However, it is important for an investor to diversify his portfolio in order to spread the risk and maintain a consistent level of profits. While this book is preparing you for penny stock trading, you do not want to exclusively stick to this type of investment alone. If your portfolio is made up of only penny stocks, it will be a very liquid asset that could change at any time. This is why having investments with long-term payoff are also important to have. But bear in mind that just diversifying will not prevent losses.

## Watch list

A watch list is what you use to keep an eye on the stocks that you have invested in. All investors need a watch list to quickly glance at how their stocks are faring. The investor need not look up the stocks every time and can simply peek at his watch list. You can have multiple watch lists in your account to distinguish between the different categories.

With modern technology, there are so many ways to do this. You can have the watch list up on your computer, or have your phone send you alerts, or even get an email if a stock goes above or below a certain amount. Some of the best apps on the market today include JStock, Bloomberg, and E*Trade, and there's even an app available through CNN. All of these apps are free to download, but some may require an account setup to work. In the long run, you will want to use one of these programs anyway, as it will help you keep better real-time track of your stocks. There are pros and cons to each of them, so make sure that you look them over well before you decide which one to go with.

## OTC

"OTC" stands for "over the counter" trading, which means using pink sheets to buy and sell stocks. As was mentioned earlier, penny stocks are not traded in stock markets because of their low prices. They are, however, traded over the counter, where certain agents have access to these stocks. All you have to do is ask the agent for the stocks that you wish to buy and they will be acquired for you. You will have to pay the agent a commission, which might be more or less the same as you would pay your regular broker or brokerage firm.

The OTC Markets Group is the most reliable company that puts out numbers for penny stocks. It publishes the values of these and other stocks that are not traded on the SEC daily and electronically on "pink sheets." This term has to do with the company's history. It were founded in 1913 as the National Quotation Bureau, and they were known for publishing the value of stocks in two different books, one on pink paper and one on yellow paper. The term "pink sheet" has stuck and now refers to stocks that are traded outside of the exchanges. In 1999, the company introduced electronic trading and stock value publishing for the very first time. The pink sheets were so well-known in the trading world that the OTC Market Group was even named

"Pink Sheets LLC" from 2000 through 2008, but it took its current name in 2010.

## Stop loss trading

Stop loss trading is a system in which a stop loss is put in place during a trade. A stop loss is nothing but a buffer that is used to safeguard an investment. You use a stop loss to prevent your investment from going bad, which is quite likely if you are dealing in penny stocks. When you pick a particular stock, you have to have a low price in mind as your stop loss price. As soon as the stock reaches that price, your deal will automatically get cancelled. Now, although you will have to settle for a loss, it will not be too large. Say, for example you bought a stock at $10. You place the stop loss at $9. Through the day, the stock keeps rising but suddenly starts dropping. It ultimately ends at $7 at the end of the trading day. Now, thanks to placing a stop loss, you were able to save $2 per share, which would be a greater loss than the $1 that you have lost. If the stop loss were not in place, you would have lost a total of $3 per share.

Such small losses are quite common in the stock market and you must not worry about them too much. You will be able to make up for the losses in the course of the day.

In order to use stop loss orders to their full advantage, you need to choose a stop loss percentage that will let the stock fluctuate a certain amount on a daily basis, while still setting it at a point that will allow you to avoid significant losses. For example, if a stock has a pattern of fluctuations of 10% or so over a week, setting your stop loss order at 5% would activate your stop loss order at a point that is well within the stock's accepted range. You would then sell your stock too early and never allow it to grow to a point where you could make a profit. Setting the stop loss order at 15% would make much more sense, as that would indicate a point low enough to avoid significant losses and high enough to allow the stock's price to fluctuate normally.

Stop loss orders are not just used to prevent losses, as they can also be used to lock in profits. This type of stop loss order is called a trailing stop loss order. With a trailing stop loss order, you set the order at a percentage level below the current market price. This allows the stop loss percentage to adjust along with the stock's market price. For example, say you decide to set your trailing stop order at 10% below the current market price, which is $20. Then the stock's price rises to $30 over a month. Your trailing stop order would be updated to set at $27 per share, which means that the least that you can earn on the share is $7.

The advantage of using stop loss orders is that you are not required to monitor the stock's performance daily, which is particularly useful in situations where you are not able to access the information for some reason. It is also helpful if you are currently trading in so many different stocks that you are not able to watch them all at the same time. If you are trying out a new stock you are nervous about, choose to watch that one closely, and use the stop loss for the stock that you are confident in and that has a predictable history.

Stop loss orders are also essentially free to implement, assuming that you set the order properly, because the commission is not paid until the order has been triggered. Perhaps the biggest advantage of stop loss orders, however, is that they remove the emotional influence from your decision-making process about whether or not to sell a stock. If you are attached to a certain stock, you may let the price drop below reason if you don't have a stop loss order in place.

The disadvantage is that stop-loss orders can be set off by a short-term change in the stock's price, which can also increase the commission fees that you pay if stop loss orders keep being executed based on the percentage that you set. Another disadvantage to keep in mind when choosing a broker to work with is that many brokers will not allow you to use stop loss orders for penny stocks. This is a question that you should ask a broker before deciding to invest with that broker.

**Intraday trading**

Intraday trading refers to trading within the day. The investor will both buy and sell the stocks within the trading day. He will not carry them forward to the next trading day and will trade them the same day regardless of the outcome. That is, he will be ready to take a loss but will want to dispose of the stocks on the same day. This is generally viewed as a positive asset that will give the investor a chance to safeguard his investments.

## Asking price, bid price, and spread

The asking price is the lowest price that a stock seller is asking from the buyer. When it comes to buying stocks, you will obviously be buying it from someone who is already holding it. That person will have a particular price in mind, which he will quote. If you are fine with the quoted price, you can agree to buy the stocks. If you wish to wait for the price to lower, you can do that as well. In the latter case, the seller's ask price will not be met.

The bid price is the highest price that someone has indicated they will pay for a stock. The spread is the difference between the asking price and the bid price. If you have ever been to an auction, you will be familiar with the idea as well. The sellers in the auction have the right to set a minimum price that needs to be reached in order for the item to be sold. If nobody bids that price, the seller retains the item. Sometimes, however, the bid price will be far greater than the sell price that has been set. This is exactly the same idea with stock trading. When buying, you must be prepared that someone may outbid you and, when selling, you may not always have someone that offers you what you want. You will then need to decide whether you want to lower your sell price or hang onto your stock a little longer until someone comes along who is willing to pay your asking price.

## Uptick and Downtick

In trading, the word "tick" is often used to refer to a trade. When a stock is traded at a higher price than was paid in the previous trade, this is called an uptick. Conversely, when the selling price is lower than in the previous trade, it is called a downtick. As a rule, multiple upticks demonstrate that a share is experiencing an upward trend, while multiple downticks show that the stock is losing value.

## Strike price

Strike price refers to the target price that a seller has in mind while disposing of stocks. He will have a particular price in mind that he expects to receive in return for the investment that's been made. Strike price varies between investments and the margin of profit also depends on the investor. Limit order is the strike price that you predetermine for your stock and mention to your customers.

Most of the time you want your strike price to be the same as your ask price, but in some situations the two will be different. Sometimes, due to high demand, you will actually get a higher return than you bargained for and outdo your strike price, while at other times you will have to make do with less.

## Volumes

"Volumes" refers to the number of buyers and number of sellers who are in the market for a particular stock. The numbers will vary as per the demand for the stock and will not remain constant. Many times, a lockdown will occur with these stocks, where the number of buyers will overtake the number of sellers by a large margin. The lockdown will only be freed the next day, when fresh orders are placed for the stocks.

When choosing which stocks to buy, you should take the volume into consideration. Depending on your strategy and the type of company you are pursuing, low or high volume may be a better option for you. You can certainly do a lot of reading on the subject, but this is one place where experience really is the best teacher. On the bright side of things, most people who have educated themselves are quick to get a feel for the market and figuring out their personal strategy.

## Market types

There are two types of markets that can exist at any given time: bearish and bullish markets. Bearish markets are known as sellers' markets, as they are marked by downward trending stock prices. Bullish markets, on the other hand, are known as buyers' markets, as they are marked by rising prices. Many reversals can take place when stock prices keep fluctuating. A bullish bar reversal comes through when the lowest price of the day is lower than the previous day's low and the current price is higher than the previous day's close. On the other hand, a bearish bar reversal is when the high is higher than the previous days and the current price is lower than the previous day's close.

Some people enjoy finding the right stocks to buy in a bearish market, when everyone else is selling, and to sell in a bullish market, when everyone else is buying. If you enjoy swimming against the current, this strategy may be for you. However, be sure to do your research so you don't end up with stocks that you regret or with a loss that is irreversible.

Remember that, with the stock market, nothing is set in stone, but you need to learn to read the indicators and warning signs.

## Stockbrokers

While using a stockbroker is not a requirement, it is certainly highly recommended, especially when you are investing in penny stocks, which can be complicated and may require specific information for proper assessment. A stockbroker is a person or a company who will carry out the actual buying and selling activity for you. You will open a trading account through your stockbroker so that your broker will be able to access the money that you have available for purchases and provide you with the money earned from any sales.

Full-service brokers offer extensive advice and investment recommendation services, but generally have high commission fees and are usually more appropriate for investors who have a lot of money to invest. These types of brokers are generally more specialized and you are less likely to have heard of them before. If you are looking to get into penny stock trading, a full-service broker is probably not what you are looking for.

The other option is a "discount" stock broker. These brokers can answer your investment questions, but will have fewer personalized services available. A discount stock broker will offer you a lower commission fee so that you make more money on your investments. Online discount brokers are an excellent option for those investing in penny stocks because you will able to check your stocks as long as you have internet access.

Some online discount stock brokers you are most likely familiar with are TD Ameritrade, Charles Schwab, and Merrill Edge. These types of brokerage services are fairly mainstream and have a proven track record. They also offer great online tools and apps that can help you keep track of your portfolio.

The main advantage of using a broker is that a broker will likely have greater access to company information, stock quotes, and other market information, which should all be provided to you free of charge if you are a client. Given the importance of collecting and assessing all available information on a company when investing in penny stocks, this is a significant advantage.

**Buy and sell orders**

A buy order is an instruction to your broker to purchase a stock that you want to acquire a share of. In order for the buy order to be processed by your broker, you will need to make sure that your trading account contains the amount of money required to cover the purchase as well as any commission fee. Most online accounts allow you to deposit money that can be held in an account and used for stock trading at any time. Time is key when stock trading, so having the funds available means one less step you have to go through before the stock you want has been sold.

A sell order is the opposite of a buy order; it is a direction to your broker to sell a stock. You will need to advise how many of your shares you want to sell, especially if you are not selling all of the shares that you own in that particular stock.

Keep in mind that most online brokerage services will not always have people available for you 24/7. However, their apps are generally extremely beneficial and include tools that can watch prices for you, alert you, and summarize your history.

## Fundamentals

This is a term that is used very frequently in the investment and trading industry. "Fundamentals" refers to various financial aspects or characteristics of a company. This includes the company's profits and losses, revenue, earnings per share, and future expectations. Think of it as the company's stats. Just as a sports team churns out statistics about all of its players, every corporation also releases numbers about its activities and well-being. You'll want to follow these stats just as closely as if you were picking football players for your fantasy football team.

## Technicals

Technicals, short for technical analysis, are another means of evaluating a company. Technicals look at a stock's patterns with respect to its share price. It is important to know whether a stock's price has been on an increasing trend or a decreasing trend, as that will be a factor you need to consider when deciding whether to purchase a stock. Knowing a stock's history is harder in the penny stock arena, as many penny stocks are newer companies that don't yet have much information available on them. Wherever possible, though, try to find at least some basic technical information.

These are the various important terms that a penny stock investor must know. You should now be able to approach just about any broker and immediately speak his or her language. Of course, other terms may come up as you delve more deeply into trading, but everything a beginner needs to know can be found above. In the next chapter we will be moving on to how to get started trading penny stocks.

# Chapter 3

# Getting Started With Penny Stocks

Now that you know all the terms, let's get you started with other basic requirements. Here are some things that you will need to trade in penny stocks successfully.

**A computer**

First is a computer. Although you can consider getting a laptop, it would be best to work with a desktop. A desktop will give you an office feeling and you won't have to worry about lugging your laptop around. You can set up an office, in fact, and prevent others from using the room.

A desktop computer is generally also more secure, because you don't take it with you to public places. If you need to trade on the go, there are plenty of apps available that will connect you to the information found on your desktop computer, so you don't need to worry about mobility. Even so, make sure that you password protect all the devices that you use for stock trading.

## Reliable connection

I cannot stress this point enough. Technology has revolutionized stock trading in the last couple of decades and online trading has become almost the exclusive method of stock trading. You cannot deal in stocks if you don't have an Internet connection. In fact, you cannot deal in penny stocks if you don't have a reliable and fast Internet connection. As you know, the penny stock market is extremely volatile and will fluctuate rapidly. If you end up missing something, you will have to settle for a loss. Every second counts in the penny stock market, so it is best to invest in a fast and reliable Internet connection.

Once again, buying and selling stocks is much like attending an auction. It requires your complete attention; otherwise an opportunity may slip through your fingers. Besides reliable Internet, it is also not a bad idea to have some sort of power backup ready. If you were to lose power, everything you were doing could be lost if you didn't save it in time and you may miss out on some great opportunities. Getting a back-up battery for your desktop computer is a cheap and easy way to avoid this problem.

## Trading account

Although you have to buy and sell penny stocks over the counter, you might still need a trading account to trade in penny stocks. For this, you can open an account in a trading firm. The firm needs to be trustworthy and you can check their background before opening up an account with them. Keep in mind that fees vary greatly from broker to broker. There are usually subtle differences in trading firm guidelines, as well, so make sure you do your research before you decide on the one you want.

The procedure to open the account is generally quite simple: You only have to fill out details and provide them with a few required documents in order to complete the legal requirements. Once your account is up and running, you can get started with the trading.

## Broker

The next step is to employ a broker, who will be able to guide you through the correct steps. This is an especially important step if you are new to penny stocks and don't know how to go about things. A broker will have access to all the right information and will be able to guide you properly. You have to find a good one, though, and do a background check if possible. Your broker should have experience and should have dealt with penny stocks. He or she should also be a qualified broker with proper certification. Going through a financial firm to find a broker is probably the best thing to do, as you will find an ideal one.

## Budget

Next, decide upon a budget. You have to set a budget that will help you invest the right amount in the market. You need to look at a sum that will be enough to get you started with penny stocks. Don't set a very high budget. Penny stocks are low-priced stocks that range between $5 and $10, which means you don't need a big budget for it. You can keep adding in money as and when you think right to do so.

This step is extremely important, as you don't want to get in over your head. Set a daily limit of what you can invest and stick to it. You should never decide to exceed your budget unless it is a special circumstance. If you are married, having a budget will also show your spouse that you are being responsible. If you want to go over your limit, talk about it first with your broker or an advisor.

## Research

You have to conduct due research on the topic in order to invest wisely. Your research should pertain to understanding the basics of penny stocks, what they can do for you, how they will contribute to your portfolio, how safe they are, etc. Besides just looking at financial news, also consider general national news. Current events can influence the market just as much as the history of a company or the state of local affairs. In short, you will need to be a well-rounded individual who keeps up with the times in order to be a successful penny stock trader.

Once you finish the basic research, you can move to researching the best stocks to invest in. Not all stocks in the penny category will be wise choices and you have to pick the ones that you think are doing well at the current moment. Once you finalize a few, you can pick out the best from that lot.

Make sure you get advice, especially when choosing your first stocks. Once you gain some experience you may also feel comfortable buying or selling stocks without consulting someone else first, but this should be the exception rather than the rule. Someone else's experience can help you just as much, if not more than your own head knowledge.

## Message boards

The next thing to consider looking into is message boards. Message boards are places where people post messages about good stocks that they wish to suggest. These suggestions are meant to help people make their decisions on which stocks to buy and which ones to avoid. You can look at which stocks are trending and which are not doing well. There will be both pumpers and bashers on the forum. The former will promote a good stock by asking people to buy it whereas the latter will bash a stock thereby bringing down its value. You have to study the boards for a while to see who is genuinely suggesting good stocks and how they are doing in the market.

Make sure that you are a part of several different types of message boards in order to get a well-rounded view of the market. Online chat groups, Facebook groups, and local community groups are great options, just to name a few.

## Journal

It is important for you to maintain a journal in order to write down all your experiences in the stock market. Keep a record of your investments from the stocks that you pick to the money invested to any other information that you think needs to be recorded. You can choose a digital or physical diary for the journal. You must dedicate yourself to making the entries in order to keep a consistent record. Looking back at the journal will help you avoid making any mistakes and remain on the right path.

Make sure you make an entry every time you sell or buy a stock. Try to organize your journal so it is easy to follow. Dividing it into sections for each type of investment, from penny stocks to precious metals, is a good place to start. Beyond that, highlight any types of stocks you seem to be doing well in. Looking at your journal, you will hopefully be able to see any emerging patterns in your successes as compared to your losses, which will help point out things that you should avoid.

These are the various things to look into when you wish to start trading in penny stocks. Armed with these tools, you are in great shape to jump right in. Next we will take a look at what exactly makes penny stocks tick.

# Chapter 4

# How Prices of Penny Stocks Are Determined

When it comes to penny stocks, many different factors can affect their rise and fall. The most basic and common ones include variations in demand and supply, news forecasts, and mergers and acquisitions.

Each of these can impact stock prices in different ways. As we already know, the theory of demand and supply varies inversely.

You can look at the number of buyers and sellers and determine whether the stock is popular or not. But do not generalize; volumes keep fluctuating all through the day and at no particular point will they remain steady unless there is a lockdown. The trick is to understand the rhythm that a particular stock follows. You will have to watch a stock carefully to understand it better. While there are specific factors that influence supply and demand, you will certainly need to learn how to sculpt your intuition, as well.

News forecasts can sometimes favor stock prices and at other times go the other way. If there is positive news about the company, its stock price will surge. On the other hand, if there is unfavorable news, the price will plummet. It has a straightforward cause-and-effect reaction, which is easy to understand. On the other hand, being in the news for positive or negative reasons can both help a company remain on top. Contrary to the adage that no news is good news, many stock market investors believe that it is best to invest in a company whose news is doing the rounds. Many people will know of the company and start buying its shares. This will mean a rise in its demand.

When listening to news you must be sure to always double-check your sources. Many stock market blunders happen due to poor news forecasts or simple misunderstandings in communication. You also need to make sure that you have the correct abbreviation for the stock that is being looked at. There are many stocks out there that have very similar abbreviations and are easily confused. This is another way in which people often make simple mistakes and buy the wrong stock.

Mergers and acquisitions also have an impact on stock prices. Say a company is doing badly and its stock prices are low. News breaks that the company getting absorbed by a Fortune 500 company. This is sure to impact the price of the stock in a positive manner. However, mergers and acquisitions are not always reason for a rise in prices, as they can also cause stock value to drop. You will need to do your homework on the merging companies to understand if it will be a beneficial undertaking in the long run or not.

These are some of the most important reasons that might cause a spike or drop in the prices of stocks. Other factors can also influence it, including even a simple rumor on the trading markets.

Let us now look at reasons that will cause penny stock prices to surge high.

**Movement in volume**

A sudden rise in the volume of stocks is a clear indication that its price is going to surge. You have to see if there is a sudden and tremendous rise in the volumes of these stocks where many buyers have queued up to get a share.

Anytime there is a waiting line, demand is high. Just as with other commodities such as food or fuel, when demand is high, prices are high. Companies will respond to demand by releasing more shares. However, it is possible for a company to overdo itself and release too many shares, so that the demand is reversed and prices plummet. Due to this risk it is better to get in on the beginning phases of this sort of rise in demand.

## Performances

You can go through a company's reports to see how they have been faring. You have to look at the results that they have published and check whether there is steady growth. If you observe that the company has surpassed its own performance in the past few years, it is reason enough for you to invest with the company.

When looking at a company's performance and income, make sure you also scrutinize the amount of debt a company holds. Some companies make the mistake of growing too quickly and running out of capital to fund their endeavors. A high debt-to-income ratio can be a warning sign. Companies with relatively low debt and high profits will be your best options.

## High highs and high lows

High highs and high lows are important to check before investing in a particular stock. As you know, you want your stocks to reach a great high and also a high low in order to help you earn big. Imagine what would happen if the stock price remained high all the time — there would be no takers for it and you would be stuck with a stock for a long time, so it is vital for stocks to plummet once in a while to help you remain invested. But these lows should not be too low and you must pick those that allow you to remain with a sizeable profit.

This can be done by looking at a company's stock price history. You will easily be able to see the normal range within which the share has stayed in the past. There are online tools that allow you to view graphs of these prices, making it easy to see at one glance whether the stock you are considering has both high highs and high lows.

## Market share

The next aspect to check is the market share of the company. As you know, having a large market share means dominating the market and having a firm foothold. When you dominate the market, you tend to leave behind the competition and also increase the pressure on parallel businesses. Investing in such a company will only benefit you and cause your stocks to increase in value over time. This piece of advice might sound strange given how penny stock companies are generally quite small in nature. However, you can pick the best ones, which will happen to be the market leaders by default.

Certainly investing in brand-new companies is also an option. Many penny stock traders enjoy this option because these stocks usually have an extremely low entry fee and don't require a large capital investment. Remember, though, that the amount of your return is limited by the amount you invest.

These are the aspects of penny stocks that you must know about before investing in order to make a lucrative investment. Understanding what makes a stock rise or fall is foundational for a positive trading experience. Now that you have an idea of what makes penny stocks tick, let's take a look at the different types of penny stocks.

*James Hawk*

# Chapter 5

# Types of Penny Stocks to Look For

You should look for particular types of stocks that will surely leave you with a large profit. Let us look at the different aspects you must consider before buying a particular penny stock.

## Companies

### *Newsworthy*

The first thing to look for is a newsworthy company, meaning one that is in the news quite often. Whether it is for positive or negative reasons, the company must remain in the headlines and provide meat for tabloids. People must take notice of it and feel the need to buy its stocks. Once there is widespread awareness and people have decided to stock up, you will have the chance to sell your stocks at a high price. However, due diligence is vital, as you must know when to invest and when to sell the stocks. The window to forge the sale might be small and you must be prepared for it.

A good guideline for the newsworthiness of a company is whether or not you have heard of the company without doing any research. Is the name of the company you are considering common knowledge or did you have to dig deep to figure out anything about this company? If information is obscure and hard to find, you will want to stay away from the company, at least until you have gained more experience in penny stock trading.

### Trustworthy

The next aspect to look for is trust. You have to be able to trust a company in order to invest in its stocks. For that, you must check its records to see that everything is clean. If there have been cases of fraud or other such malfeasance, you must steer clear of the company. If the company has a great track record, it will be great to invest with. However, don't expect to see a squeaky clean record, as that will not exist. There might be a few glitches in the company's report that you must ignore if you want to invest in a good stock.

Besides just looking into the legal history of a company, also take a look at their current numbers, paying attention to detail. Most companies will put out at least a quarterly report for its shareholders. Make sure that nothing seems suspicious. Of course, the ultimate trust of a company comes if you personally know those in the leadership, but that will only very rarely be the case. Even then, make sure that personal emotions are not clouding your judgment.

### Well-to-do

You have to look for well-to-do companies that are making sizeable profits. Some companies will make consistent profits owing to their amazing business sense. You must know that Microsoft started out as a penny stock company and those that invested in it during the initial stages have turned into millionaires; so you have to assess the true value of a company in regard to its profits. Find a company that shows consistent growth and profits in the past and chances are it will continue on that trend in the future.

*James Hawk*

## Future growth

You must also assess the future growth of a company. You have to see if the company will turn bigger in the future and establish a place for itself. Although it is tough to make such an assessment based on the company's current performance, you can at least estimate the path that the company will take in the future. Once you think you have a company that is going to do well, you can consider investing in it.

A big factor for future growth is innovation. Those companies that do not innovate are one day doomed to fail. There are many companies that used to be huge but failed to innovate and have since decreased in stature. Think, for example, about AOL, Kodak, and Blockbuster. All of these companies used to be household names, but due to progression in technology (e.g., digital cameras, online movie streaming, and Netflix), these companies are basically obsolescent because they failed to innovate and adapt to the changes around them. If a company is to have future growth, they need to be willing to innovate.

## Industry

It is well-established knowledge that there are certain industries in which companies have penny stocks for trading. The mining and metals industry, for example, is particularly well-known for how many companies it has that trade in penny stocks. The same goes for companies within the commodity business and the online tech development sector. When an industry tends to have more of these companies that operate in penny stocks, this means that the companies are more likely to have experience with this type of share structure. So investment in these companies is probably a safer and more reliable option.

## Positive earnings or contracts

If a company has positive revenue, it is always a good sign that it is at least headed in the right direction. Having a lucrative contract with another company –especially a higher-value company – is another excellent indicator that a company is on the right track. For example, an egg product company may have long-term contracts with both an egg supplier and numerous packaging facilities that buy their product. If these contracts are long-term, it is very likely that the company will at least remain stable, if not show considerable growth. While you cannot simply rely on the information provided by the company itself about its revenue or contracts, if you are able to verify the information through an independent source, you should consider investing in the company.

It is important to keep in mind, though, that a positive earnings report does not automatically mean that a stock's price is going to rise, and a negative earnings report does not necessarily mean that the stock price will decrease. There are many other factors that will impact the stock price of a company. You may want to hold off on trading a stock just before or right around the earnings report release because it could help to see how others are reacting before you decide whether to invest in that particular company.

### *Recent financing*

If a penny stock company has just gone through the financing process with an established lender at or around the current share price, this is a good indication that investors are taking the company seriously and are looking at it as a relatively solid investment opportunity. The more capital that a company is able to raise, and the more well-established and reputable that the lender is, the more likely it is that the financing is a sign of positive growth and potential success.

Remember, though, that too much debt can also be a negative thing. Think of your own personal credit. You need to have some loans in order to build a healthy credit score, but if your credit balances are maxed out and are not being paid off, but merely maintained, your credit rating will suffer. This same principle can be applied to the health of a company's financial assets.

Financing can be a negative indicator in another way as well. If a company completes a financing deal at a significant discount to the current market price, this is a sign that the company is desperate, which is obviously not beneficial for investors and for the future success of the company. Doing additional research into the details of the financing deal and why the company needed financing will help you to decide whether the financing is a positive or negative sign for the company.

## New partnerships

Even if the partnership itself is not particularly significant, just the fact that a partnership has been announced will tend to positively impact a company's stock price, because it is an indication that another company is interested in the first company and sees it as at least a potentially viable partner. If you keep an eye on upcoming partnerships, you may be able to purchase the stock before the partnership is well-known and make a significant profit on your investment. If multiple companies are competing for a partnership with a particular company, that company is most likely to be very strong and healthy, and investing in it would be a good idea.

## News about the overall industry

Generally speaking, if an industry has a positive news announcement, the stock of companies within that industry will rise as a result of expectations. Examples, where this has occurred, include marijuana penny stock companies when marijuana was legalized in some states. The share prices of penny stock companies that operate within the marijuana industry rose as a result of the news. Any investor who had shares in the companies prior to the announcement almost certainly earned a profit once the announcement of legalization was made.

Just as with positive news, if there is an announcement that negatively affects an industry, the companies within that industry will likely be negatively impacted. Even negative rumors can have an impact. They may not be officially released in the news, but if word gets around that an industry is in trouble, this will make its way into trading. The news or rumors may not have anything to do with the specific company that you are looking at, but it could still impact a specific company. This can be a good time to purchase stocks if you believe that the negative impact will be short-term.

Another type of news that can impact certain sectors is a natural disaster. An area that has been hit by a tornado, flood, or something similar, may hurt the insurance industry, while at the same time the construction industry will experience a resurgence. Predicting these types of behaviors can help you decide what industry you want to look at for your investments at the time.

## Changes in management

While a change in management is not always an indication that there is trouble brewing for a company, it is generally safe to assume that a management change is a bearish sign for a stock. Realistically, if a company's management is doing well and the company is profiting, there is rarely a reason for management to be changed. It is probably a good idea to avoid investing in companies that are undergoing, or have recently undergone, a change in management. You should instead wait until things have settled and you can determine whether this change is good for this particular company or not.

## FDA approval and lawsuits

Companies that are involved with any kind of FDA approval process or lawsuit should usually be avoided as an investment opportunity. If a company applies for FDA approval and the approval is granted, that can make the share price skyrocket. However, if the approval is rejected, the share price can drop drastically.

The factor that makes investing in companies involved in the FDA approval process particularly risky is that any trading in the stock will be put on pause before the FDA's decision is announced, so you will not be able to respond quickly and cut your losses if the FDA rejects the application. Given the very high potential risk, it is probably not worth it to invest in companies involved in the FDA process unless you have weighed the pros and cons and decided that the high risk is acceptable within your investment plan and investment rules.

Companies that are involved in lawsuits have a similar issue: While winning a court case can certainly have a positive impact on a company's share price, losing (or getting involved in the first place) will almost always cause the share price to drop. There is also the risk that a judge hearing the matter will make some negative comment about the company, which could also impact the share price of the company. As with companies going through the FDA approval process, it is usually better to avoid companies involved in lawsuits and to choose a safer investment option.

This idea can also be extended to companies that are impacted by government regulation. This is yet another reason why staying up to date with current news is so important. For example, if a new law is put in place that requires consumption of electricity to move to renewable energy for a certain percentage amount, you can expect growth in that market sector. At the same time, you can expect conventional companies to lose value.

## Stocks

The number of stocks a company releases can impact its value. If a company suddenly decides to double the number of shares available, but there is no demand to meet this move, you can expect the value of the shares to drop drastically. On the other hand, if there is a waiting line for the particular company's stocks, which we have already mentioned previously, an increase in share amounts can only help.

### *Market share*

The first and best type of stock to look for is one that has a large market share. As was mentioned earlier, market share plays a big part in telling whether a company is doing well or not. If it has a big market share, it is bound to do well, as there will be a lot of investors holding the company's shares. You can call the company's customer cell and enquire about its market share to get an idea of it. You will be surprised at the number of well-known companies who are still trading as penny stocks.

### Undervalued stocks

Undervalued stocks are the most sought-after stocks in the world. These are the stocks of companies that are waiting to boom. Say, for example, you do some calculation to see the true value of a stock and find out that it is being undervalued in the market. You quickly buy it, knowing that it will reach its true value at one point or the other. This will surely help you remain with a sizeable profit. Now repeat with the next set of undervalued stocks and so on and so forth.

To do this successfully, you need to have your finger on the pulse of the stock market. You will need to put your bargain-hunting skills into use when trying to find these undervalued stocks. The thing that makes undervalued stocks a very secure investment is that these types of stocks almost always belong to reliable and stable companies.

### Will not drop lower

The next type of penny stocks to consider is those that will not drop any lower but will possibly remain at the same level as they are at or keep rising steadily. When you invest in such a stock, you are sure to capitalize on its capacity to not fall any lower. Don't think such stocks will be readily waiting for you. You have to do some research to find them in order to invest. Once you invest, you must remain patient.

With these types of stocks you basically have nothing to lose. If you invest only a few cents per share, your investment will be relatively low and your risk almost non-existent. At the same time, great reward is possible. If, for example, you had gotten in on the ground floor investing in Google, your investment would have grown by over 1500%.

### Pride stocks

Pride stocks are those that will make you proud to own them. They may belong to companies that are quite popular. Don't worry; not all penny stock companies are small and unknown. You will surely find some that are doing well and add pride to your portfolio holdings. Such stocks will surely grow in value over the course of time and leave you with a great profit. Be careful, however, not to misplace your pride.

## Dividends

It is possible to find penny stocks that pay dividends, although they are not common. You can look for newsletters and websites that offer information about penny stocks. These will often tell you which penny stocks offer dividends.

A dividend is paid when a company distributes its profits among its shareholders instead of reinvesting them in the business. Often companies will have a payment schedule that they adhere to and this is no different for penny stocks. The difficulty with penny stocks is that the turnaround time is generally so quick that dividends are never received.

You can also use an online stock screener, which is an instrument used by traders and investors to filter stocks based on metrics as defined by the user. There are many free online stock screeners available, and they will allow you select the criteria that are important to you when choosing the penny stocks in which you would like to invest. Criteria on which you can base your choices include market capitalization, dividend yield, price, and average 5-year ROI (return on investment). An online stock screener is a more direct and efficient way to find penny stocks that pay dividends and that meet with any other requirements that you have set.

Due to the high-risk nature of penny stocks, finding those that pay dividends can help to maximize and preserve your investment capital, and therefore reduce the overall investment risk. Even if your penny stock's price stays stagnant for a year, you will still earn an annual dividend that will improve your overall profit/loss position.

These are the various aspects to look for in a penny stock or company before buying. Now that you have a better idea of what exactly makes penny stocks rise and fall in value and which types of stocks you should keep an eye out for, let's talk about how you can learn to predict the ups and downs in penny stock value.

# Chapter 6

# Price Prediction in Penny Stocks

It is important to predict the price trends of penny stocks, as they can be quite volatile. You surely don't want to end up with one that fluctuates unpredictably, as that can leave your investment in a rut.

There are many prediction techniques that you can use to determine how a particular stock will move. In this chapter, we will look at some of the most popular and widespread methods.

## Candlesticks

Candlesticks trading is a type of analysis in which people place candlesticks on a graph that contains the highs and lows of a particular stock's price. This will help determine the course that the stock will take and allow the person to make the right move. Candlesticks analysis requires the person to thoroughly understand the mathematical calculations that go into it. If you are not adept at math, you might find it a little difficult to go ahead with candlestick calculations.

If you do put the time and effort into learning how to read one of these graphs, it can be of great help to you. One quick glance can tell you all that you need to know about a certain stock, and you won't need to spend time doing difficult calculations and analyses on your own.

## Fibonacci series

Fibonacci numbers are numbers in a mathematical series that follows a pre-determined route. It is frequently found in nature in the form of concentric circles, such as on a seashell or a fiddlehead. You can calculate the next price where the stock will stop based on the number series. But remember that you have to know how to calculate it in order to carry out this method successfully. You can use the help of someone who is good in math. However, you must not allow any scope for error as that might give you wrong results.

Many people claim to have been very successful using this method; however, there are still quite a few skeptics out there who insist the whole idea is a sham. Only personal experience can tell you whether this method is something you should consider for yourself.

## Trend following

This is just what it sounds like: following the dominant trend. That is, if all the stocks in the particular category are rising, you assume that the one you have picked to invest in will also rise. On the other hand, if everything is falling, the one you have picked will also fall. It is simple enough to understand this bit, but what is tough to know is whether the one you have picked will compulsorily follow the trend that the others are following. There is no way of knowing this unless you give it a try. Of course you won't experience 100% results. That does not occur anywhere, except if you have truly cracked the code to investing.

Some investors prefer to try to set trends instead of follow them, but this is a much riskier undertaking. If you have gained enough experience so you are comfortable with this, give it a try, but beginners should avoid it.

## News forecasts

News forecasting is picking stocks based on news articles. As you know, some favorable news might break out about a company that will allow you to make the right investments. And, if bad news breaks, you will know to stay away from the stock or sell it at the earliest. Either way, you will have to follow the news to do the right thing.

While there are great apps for trading, there are also apps available that can keep you in touch with the latest news as soon as it is released. You can set alerts to target specific industry sectors, just as you can set trading apps to alert you about certain stocks.

## Price actions

"Price actions" refers to looking at the graph of a stock and seeing when it rises and when it falls during a month. The investor will then assume that the stock will follow the same pattern the next month as well and will be prepared for the outcome. This is quite an effective method to follow and one that is sure to leave you with a guaranteed profit, provided you observe the trend keenly. You must not be in a hurry or jump to conclusions about the stocks. This method can only be used on well-established companies that have a past history, so for new companies you will have to find a different method that works best for you.

## Swing trading

Swing trading is another type of trading that you can use: The investor puts a stop loss in place and wait for the price to rise. If it falls, the stop loss will check it. Now, the investor will assume a fresh position from the same place, so as to bring in a profit. In other words, you are buying and selling the same stock multiple times in a row. This might seem strange but it is a trend that many old hands follow to remain with profits at the end.

## Contrarian trading

Contrarian trading is the opposite of trend following. Here, the investor will assume the opposite will happen in terms of the price. For example, if it is rising, he thinks that it will fall anytime. And, if the prices are rising, he thinks that they will rise at any time. He will also invest with the contrarian mindset and buy those stocks that are falling and sell the ones that are rising. This is also a very strange concept but it's what investment greats like Warren Buffet are said to follow.

## Rebate trading

In rebate trading, people use ECNs to carry out trade. ECNs are electronic communication networks. These are networks that require a certain number of investors to invest with them and set up an artificial network. These traders will deal within these circuits and the hosts will be paid based on the number of investors that have invested with them. The benefit of these types of groups is that they spread out the risk among multiple groups and stocks, making your individual risk smaller.

## Range trading

Range trading refers to trading within a range. The investor will look for a stock that will rise and fall within the same range. Say for example a penny stock will rise to $10 and fall to $2. That is the absolute range that it will follow, which will make it easy for you to predict the trend. This will also help you invest within a specified range. One benefit of this is that it allows you to budget more easily, as you know the exact range of money you may be investing.

## Software

You can also use software to predict the trend that the stock will follow. These are better known as artificial intelligence systems that will help you predict the trends that the stocks will follow. You may have to buy the software. Some programs are even somewhat automated, taking the stress of buying and selling at exactly the right moments off your shoulders.

These are the various ways in which you can predict the trends that penny stocks will follow. You will also gain experience and intuition the more you trade. Each trader eventually comes up with his or her own formula that works best and has shown them positive results in the past. Next we will take a look at different techniques that can be used in order to analyze penny stocks.

*James Hawk*

# Chapter 7

# Penny Stock Analysis Techniques

Analyzing stocks is very important. You have to analyze them through different lenses to see if they make good investment vehicles. In this chapter, we will look at the basic types of analysis that you can use.

## Fundamental analysis

Fundamental analysis is the analysis of the basic financial health of the company. You will have to acquire and go through some important documents. At a minimum, reputable companies will at least put out a quarterly report. However, many companies chose to keep their shareholders informed even more frequently than that, on a monthly or biweekly basis. Most of these reports are open to the public. If you cannot find them, you can certainly request a copy from the company in question.

### Income statement

This method requires understanding in detail all the income that you receive on a monthly basis through your company. As you know, it can come in the form of operating and non-operating incomes. Operating income is what the company earns by selling the products and services they produce, so it is a direct result of their work that earns them their operating income. On the other hand, non-operating income refers to money that the company earns by means other than product and service sales, so a company can earn non-operating income by selling its possessions such as furniture, televisions etc. If you spot something unusual, such as the company selling a lot of their possessions all at once, it might indicate a financial crisis that they are going through. You must further investigate it before making an investment.

### Balance sheet

The balance sheet is a very common financial document that any company maintains to showcase their company's health. A balance sheet helps record many calculations, such as debts that they owe, liabilities that they have, assets that they own, etc. As the name indicates, a balance sheet shows all of these different aspects of the company on a balanced summary, with the income and expense sides balancing out to the same number. When you go through these numbers, you must check if the company has enough assets to counteract the liabilities. If they don't, it means that their stocks will not work well in the long run. On the other hand, if the company has a lot of assets and just a few liabilities, it is a good company to invest with. Remember that companies put out balance sheets every quarter and you have to go through all of them.

### Cash flow statement

This is a statement that indicates the total amount of cash that is flowing in and out of the company. A cash flow statement shows the expenses and income that the company has. Based on those two figures, you can tell if a company is faring well or not. A cash flow statement is a great tool to use when you wish to understand the financial health of a company. As opposed to a balance sheet, a cash flow statement is shown in a chronological format. This can be helpful, as it gives you a better idea if there are any rhythms that the company follows. Looking at this report, you can find out if there is a particular time of year in which buying or selling stock would be the most profitable.

These are the different legal papers that you have to go through to check the overall financial health of the company. If you think the company is doing well financially, you can consider investing in it, but not before going through its technical details.

## Technical analysis

The next type of analysis is known as technical analysis, which deals with understanding the trends that a stock will follow based on the trends that it has been following in the past.

Obviously, you will have to go through the trends to analyze and understand them effectively. Here are the different types of trends that you have to study when considering a stock.

### *Direction*

The very first thing to look at is the direction in which the stock is moving. Stocks usually move in a predisposed position, which might be up or down. If your stock is moving up and down within equal intervals, it is a good stock to pick. Balanced stocks make for great investment choices. But if your stock has reached its peak point when you plan on investing, you must be careful as its price might start to fall down. You will be running a risk by investing in something that has reached an all-time high. On the other hand, if the stock has reached a low point, chances are high that it will start to rise, so it would be great for you to invest in such a stock. However, remember that neither of these assumptions might turn out to be true, which means that it is tough to generalize. You have to observe several graphs in order to understand price behavior. Graphs such as the candlestick graph can be a great indicator of what direction a stock is going in and when the best time for buying or selling would be.

## Speed

The next thing to check is the speed at which the stocks are moving. All stocks will move up and down at a particular speed. This speed determines whether the stock is heading up or down and how fast will it reach the two extreme points.

You can draw 4 points on the graph that will stand for waves 1, 2, 3, and 4. These will help you read the graph better and understand how the trend is occurring.

Now suppose wave 1 and wave 4 are overlapping. This means that the stock is undergoing a correction phase and the two will experience similar values. Most people wait out correction phases in order to allow the price to settle down.

If you think a stock has moved up too fast, you must understand that it will also fall back down just as fast. This can be a telltale sign that the stock is extremely volatile and you must invest in it with caution. Penny stocks are known for this sort of rapid change, so you will first want to try your hand on some more reliable stocks. However, with experience, even speedy stocks can be invested in successfully.

### Distance

The next aspect to check is the distance that the stock has covered. It is possible for a stock to surpass its all-time high and keep breaking records. This mainly happens when favorable news about the company breaks out. You will see that the stock is moving higher and higher and then stagnates at a high point. On the other hand, a stock can also move the other way and reach an all-time low. This is most likely when some unfavorable news has broken about the company and the price of the stock is going downward.

## *Chart patterns*

Reading a stock's chart pattern takes into consideration the technical analysis factors discussed above. There are certain frequent patterns that can be very useful indicators as to the strength and viability of a company for investment purposes.

If you keep a detailed journal and enjoy swing trading, creating your own charts may also be a valuable asset to your penny stock endeavor. Any types of charts or graphs are extremely helpful, as they tell you in one glance what words would take a paragraph or more to explain.

## *Clean chart*

A clean chart is one where there is a very clear trend in the pattern of the stock's share price. Either the share price has consistently decreased or consistently increased. It is recommended that you always stick to investing in companies with clean charts because it is much easier to read the trends and make an educated decision as to whether the company is a good investment.

Each of the chart patterns discussed in this section has a messy counterpart. Overall, a messy chart is unhelpful because it does not provide a pattern that will offer a reasonable analysis of the company's share price history and therefore will not assist in predicting future share price trends. Charts that portray trends and averages will always be better than charts that are too detailed to do so. After all, with a chart the goal is to see the forest, not the trees.

Clean bullish

If the trend shows an increase in share prices, this is a bullish trend and is a positive indicator of the financial strength of the company. Be aware of stocks that have bullish trends that are too clean, though, as this can be an indication that there may be some manipulating of the company's share price going on.

Clean bearish

When a company's share price has decreased consistently, this is called a clean bearish trend. Generally, this will be an indication that the company is not doing well financially, and you may wish to avoid investing in such a company. On the other hand, a company that has a clean bearish trend can be a great opportunity for short-selling if you are interested in that type of activity.

## Clean breakout

A clean breakout chart shows a company's share price fluctuating within a fairly well-established range, followed by a sudden sharp increase. For anyone interested in penny stock trading, this type of pattern is perfect because, if you purchase shares just as the breakout is starting, you can make a significant profit.

## Clean breakdown

As with the clean breakout chart, in a clean breakdown chart, the share's price will fluctuate within a fairly consistent range until there is suddenly a significant decrease. A breakdown can be the result of negative news about a company, or some other event that causes investors to want to sell their stock. If a company's stock starts to break down, you should probably consider selling unless you have reason to believe that the breakdown will be temporary.

However, a breakdown can also sometimes be the result of stop loss orders. If a company's share price fluctuates within a fairly well-established range, there will probably be a fairly clear appropriate stop loss order point that will be chosen by many investors. If the share price happens to hit that point, all of those stop loss orders will be activated because it is an automatic process. Once that occurs, the share price will decrease even further because of the sudden mass exodus of investors.

If you look at a company's chart and see either a clean breakout or a clean breakdown, do some (quick) research into the possible reasons behind the change and decide whether it is a good time to sell or buy, as applicable.

<u>Clean cup and handle</u>

While this may sound like a table setting, a company with a clean cup and handle chart can potentially be a great investment opportunity if you play it right. A cup and handle pattern is when a company's share price rises and then falls over a fairly short period, after an extended period rises again into a breakout. If you time it right, purchase the stocks at the correct time, and wait it out long enough, you can make a substantial profit when the second price rise occurs.

<u>Clean double top</u>

A clean double top chart pattern is essentially the same as the cup and handle, but in the double top there is no breakout of the share price – it simply increases significantly but within the fluctuation trends of the stock. As with the cup and handle, if you time your sale of the stock properly, you can earn significant revenue from this investment.

In addition to these, there are many other things that you can look into, such as the general trend that the stock is following on a monthly basis that will tell you when it will rise and dip. Having proper knowledge about this will help you predict stocks well and invest safely.

Remember that the fundamental and technical analyses are on two different planes, which do not converge. This means that a fundamental analyst need not necessarily be a technical analyst and vice versa. If you wish to properly understand how the company is going, you will have to indulge in both these types.

Hopefully this chapter has helped you understand the different ways in which you can analyze penny stocks to help you improve upon your investments. In the next chapter, we will be taking a look at trading penny stocks as a day trading process.

# Chapter 8

# Penny Stock Day Trading

In this chapter, we will look at what day trading stands for and why you should day trade with penny stocks. Day trading really is the easiest way to break into the penny stock world, and we hope this chapter helps you do just that.

## What is day trading?

Day trading refers to trading that occurs within a single day. The investor will buy and sell stocks within the same day and not hold on to them, even if it means settling for a loss.

Now you may wonder why the trader is keen on disposing of the stocks when he can hold on to them for a while longer and ring in a profit.

The answer is quite simple: The trader is not interested in allowing his investment to remain where it will not prove to be a lucrative choice. He is better off taking a loss at that point in time than a profit on it sometime later, which will eventually prove to be a bigger loss.

For example, let's say an investor has bought 100 stocks worth $2 each. He has made an investment of $200, which he hopes to increase to $250 by end of the day. However, the per stock value drops to $1.5 at the end of the day, meaning that he has to settle for a loss.

The trader will agree to take the loss and will not hold the stock unnecessarily. Even if the stock moves to $2 the next day, he will not bother about it.

In most cases, day traders have a high margin for losses, so they will not be worried about losing a few hundred dollars a day.

They will also set themselves high margins, which will counteract the losses. It is obvious that the ratio between the two will have to differ by a large margin, especially if the investor wishes to remain with hefty profits.

As you already know, penny stock traders try to earn a big profit by combining several small profits that they earn all through the day. A penny stock day trader will only be able to make a big profit if he selects 10 or 12 good stocks that will rise in value in the course of the day to leave him with a profit.

Not all day traders are penny stockholders, mind you, so it is not an exclusive feature of penny stock traders alone. There will be many other investors in the ring who will hold the same stocks for, possibly, a much longer time.

## Why should you day trade in penny stocks?

Now coming to the main debate, why should penny stocks be traded on a daily basis? Well, there are many reasons for it and we will look at them in detail.

First off, as you already know, penny stocks are quite volatile and will keep moving up and down all through the day. A trader can earn a better profit if he holds the stocks for a single day than by holding them for several days. He will be wasting both his money and his effort, as the same stock will give him bigger profits if he buys it fresh every single day.

When you trade on a daily basis, you have the chance to know how much you are worth and don't have to wait another day to know your true worth. This is great for all those that wish to know exactly how much they have in their holding and plan their next investment.

A person considerably cuts down on the risk of an investment going bad by selling it off on the same day. The stock might never recover soon enough and you will be stuck with a headache that you will want to get rid of at the earliest opportunity.

Many companies that charge hefty brokerage fees for transactions generally double it when it comes to holding stocks for more than a day. They will make you pay a hefty sum for holding stocks of companies overnight.

It is also important to note that penny stock companies can wind up without a notice. They will be small companies making marginal profits and, if they deem it fit to wind up instead of continuing, your investment will be in danger. Even if they give you buffer time to sell stocks, if nobody buys them from you, your investment is sure to get stuck in a rut, so it is important for you to be well informed about the companies and not risk leaving behind an overnight investment.

These are some of the reasons why penny stocks are best traded within a single day. But it is surely not limited to just these. There can be many other reasons that make investors pick day trading as the best method to trade in penny stocks.

You can try out both day trading and holding techniques when it comes to penny stocks and use the one that works best for you. Remember that individual stocks require individual treatment and it would be wrong to generalize about anything.

Remember that you don't always have to day trade with penny stocks and can trade normally as well. Many prefer to do day trading because they see it as an opportunity to capitalize on a stock's ability to move up and down within a limited period of time.

By now you should have a great foundational knowledge for trading with penny stocks. We've looked at the different types of stocks, how to predict their behavior, what to look for in analysis, and how to day trade. Now let's take a moment to look at some general dos and don'ts of penny stocks.

# Chapter 9

# Dos and Don'ts of Penny Stocks

In this chapter, we will look at the various dos and don'ts of penny stock trading to help you understand the concept better.

## Dos of penny stocks
<u>Do read up</u>

It is extremely important for you to be well informed about your stocks, so make sure that you read up about them regularly. There is nothing like having enough knowledge on a topic; you must read as much as possible and then read some more. You have to keep reading up on a topic until you think you have enough knowledge to invest bravely. You can look up information on the Internet and also read books that will help your cause.

## Do consider the downs

It is extremely important to consider the downside of penny stocks as well, especially if you wish to invest in it long term. Having just one half of a picture will not give you a clear idea of what it looks as a whole. You have to put in the effort to take everything into consideration before making your final choice. If you think it is best for you to avoid investing in penny stocks because you will not be able to control it, you can give it some more time.

## Do have a plan in mind

When it comes to trading in penny stocks, you have to have a foolproof plan in mind. There is no point in getting into something without having a valid blueprint for it. You run the risk of getting lost and might also lose money. Therefore, the wise thing to do would be to have a plan that will allow you to invest your money in all the right avenues. Sit down with someone who is good at investments and make the plan. Your plan should change every now and then, as keeping it a constant might not get you the desired results.

## Do set rules for yourself

Along with your investment plan, you should set rules for yourself about your investments. Know how much you are willing to lose, the types of companies that you are willing to invest in, and the fundamentals that a company must have before you will purchase its stock. And, most important, stick to these rules! Penny stock trading, like any other trading, can move pretty quickly and sometimes quick decisions may need to be made. Following your rules will help you avoid making a decision that you might regret later.

## Do commit to working hard

As is discussed throughout this book, research is an absolutely essential component of successful investing in penny stocks. If you are not willing to make the commitment to doing the research that is necessary for you to obtain the information that you need, you should not get involved with penny stocks. While your broker will be able to provide you with information, you should still do your own research as well. This includes researching companies, reading press releases, and reviewing your investments so that you know whether their status is satisfactory or you need to think about selling. Trading in penny stocks is not about making a quick and easy buck. It takes time and hard work but, if done correctly, it can make you a substantial profit.

## Do accept that you will make mistakes

You are going to make mistakes, and you are going to incur losses. This reality does not apply only to penny stock trading, but to any type of investment strategy. Those mistakes will hurt, but they will also teach you valuable lessons. Which brings up another do and a related don't: do learn from your mistakes, and do not repeat them. As the expression goes, "fool me once, shame on them; fool me twice, shame on me." Making a mistake once is acceptable and to be expected, but making that same mistake again is an unnecessary cost and could become very discouraging. Help yourself by paying attention to where you went wrong and avoiding those same decisions in the future.

## Do keep your goals in mind

Investing can be very exciting, especially if your stocks are doing well. But you should always keep your goals in mind and why you wanted to start investing in the first place. If you have a specific intended purpose for any money that you make, keeping that purpose in mind will help you to stay on track by motivating you when you experience a setback, or when the investment industry seems too overwhelming or complicated. It can also help to keep your head on straight if you have a stock that suddenly earns a substantial profit. It might be tempting to keep the stock in the hope that its price will rise even further, but you will need to consider whether that is the best approach for you and your goals, or whether it would be better to sell the stock and take the guaranteed profits at the moment.

## Do adopt stop loss

It is important for you to have a stop loss strategy to help you safeguard your investments. You must know by now what a stop loss strategy refers to. It deals with choosing a low point where the price of the stock might stop. Once it hits that mark, you will automatically be thrown out of the game. This is a great strategy to adopt and what every amateur investor must do, especially during the initial investments.

## Do take share structure into consideration

The share structure of a company – i.e. the number of shares that it has and how those shares are classified – is an important factor to consider when deciding which companies you to invest in. When a company chooses to exercise its right to issue employee stock options, carry out stock splits, or issue shares to raise capital, that can dilute your investment. The more outstanding shares that a company has, the smaller percentage you own of the company. This can have a positive impact on your investment if the dilution ends up making the company more profitable, but you will want to consider this factor when deciding whether to purchase or keep penny stocks.

Look at the company's share structure both currently and historically. If a company has experienced several bouts of dilution of its shares, you may want to avoid investing in that company.

## Do invest wisely

You have to invest wisely, as the stock market can be a very tricky place. If you think your investments will go bad, you must exercise precaution and do whatever is necessary to safeguard your money. Wise investment need not always translate to overnight riches. It can also mean making moves that will help you remain invested in something for a long time and your money's worth will keep increasing on a daily basis.

## Don'ts of penny stocks

In the previous segment we looked at some of the dos of stock market trading and in this segment we will look at the don'ts.

## Don't blindly follow

You have to stop yourself from blindly following what someone else is doing. You must have an action plan of your own that will allow you to convert your money into wealth. Do not apply the same strategy that someone else is applying, as it might not work for you the same way. You must have an individual approach to your own investing game and something that might not work for someone else.

You can turn to others for advice but do not rely on them to formulate an investment plan for you.

## Don't get discouraged

Don't get discouraged by your initial losses, as they will not last long. Many new investors feel nervous when they suffer a loss and they wonder if they will lose all their money in the stock market. But only the wise will take a lesson from their loss and ensure that they don't repeat the same mistake again. It is ideal for you to maintain a journal in which you can record all the transactions on a daily basis. You can then look back at it to see the trend that you have been following in terms of stock market investments.

## Don't believe everything you read

Many investors subscribe to newsletters that are sent by random websites that provide advice on stocks. But it is a mistake to believe what they have to say and blindly invest in their stocks. You have to do your own research and stop trusting others too much. If you get a tip from somewhere, then study it first instead of blindly going with it. You can also refer to message boards if you like and pick stocks but beware of pump and dump stocks that some pumpers might have laid out as a trap for investors.

## Don't expect overnight riches

This is one bad habit that many people fall prey to. They expect overnight riches and think they can turn their hundreds into millions. This is, however, impossible, as nobody can become rich overnight. Have reasonable goals in mind, such as 2 or 5 years. That is an ideal timeline to earn a substantial amount from your investments.

## Don't have bad network

Do not have a bad network connection when you wish to invest in the stock market. As you know, stock prices vary on a minute-to-minute basis and, if you have a bad connection, you might lose out on a lucrative deal. This might sound extremely rudimentary but it is one of the most important aspects that an investor must bear in mind.

## Don't fall into 'penny-baited traps'

As discussed in Chapter 1, there tends to be a lack of useful information for investors when it comes to penny stocks and they often have low liquidity. Aside from making penny stocks a somewhat riskier proposition, this also makes them an easy target for people looking to commit fraud. There are a lot of scams that fraudsters use to dupe investors, with a few that are particularly common.

The use of biased recommendations is a common scam used by fraudsters. Some penny stock companies will actually pay people to make recommendations about the company throughout various forms of media, including financial television and radio shows, newsletters, and spam emails. Any time that you receive a recommendation about a penny stock from any source other than the dominant media platforms, you must investigate further to make sure that the individual making the recommendation is in no way connected to the penny stock company.

Another scam that is often used is when a penny stock company sells its stock to offshore brokers in order to avoid having to register its stock. The sale to the offshore brokers is often done at a discount as an incentive to the offshore broker. The offshore broker will then turn around and sell the stock to U.S. investors at a profit that is significantly higher than what the offshore broker paid in the first place. In addition, offshore brokers will often use what is known as "boiler room" sales methods to convince investors to purchase the stock.

"Boiler room" tactics are when a broker employs salespeople (essentially telemarketers) to telephone lists of potential investors and provide only positive information about the stocks that the broker is selling. Any negative information will be ignored or minimized and the potential investors will be discouraged from doing their own research into the stock and pressured into making the purchase right away. It is estimated by the North American Securities Administrators Association that investors lose $10 billion per year to this type of investment fraud.

<u>Don't believe the penny stock fallacy</u>

The penny stock fallacy encapsulates two erroneous beliefs: that many or most of the blue chip stocks today started as penny stocks, and that there is automatically a positive correlation between the quantities of stocks owned by an investor and that investor's returns.

Many people mistakenly believe that the high-value, blue-chip stocks of today, such as Microsoft or Wal-Mart, must have started out as penny stocks. This belief is often the result of looking at the stocks' adjusted stock price, which takes into consideration stock splits. Stock splits are when a company decides to divide its shares to create more shares. The price per share goes down accordingly, so the overall valuation is not impacted, but it does allow for stocks to be priced lower and therefore attract more investors.

Although the adjusted stock price, taking into consideration stock split, may show that a blue-chip company's stock price value was quite low on their first day of trading, this does not mean that the stock was actually a penny stock. In fact, the overall value of the company may have been quite high, requiring the company to divide its shares so that more people could purchase shares.

As for the positive correlation between the amount of stocks owned and your return, that correlation can exist, but it should not be assumed or taken for granted. If a penny stock is priced at 10 cents and the price rises by 5 cents, you have earned a 50% return. So the percentage of return can rise quite quickly. However, this percentage of return does not automatically reflect the overall value of your stocks; the stock is still only valued at 15 cents. Also, given that penny stocks often are not successful, the probability of losing the entire investment is high.

## Don't forget valuation when looking at share price

A common mistake made by amateur and beginner investors is assuming that penny stocks are more affordable simply because of the share price. Just because you are getting more shares in a company for a lesser cost does not automatically mean that it is a better investment. You need to take into consideration the company's overall valuation when you are selecting the penny stocks in which you will invest. In order to do this, find out how many outstanding shares the company has.

"Outstanding shares" means the company's stock as currently held by all of its shareholders. To determine the number of outstanding shares that a company has, look at the heading "capital stock" on the company's balance sheet. The number of outstanding shares will impact the company's valuation, also called its market capitalization.

For example, if Company X has a share price of $0.10 and Company Y has a share price of $100, you might think that you are getting a better deal because you can buy 1000 shares in Company X for $100 while you can only buy 1 share in Company Y for the same price. However, if both companies have 100,000 shares, Company Y's market capitalization ($10 million) is substantially better than Company X's ($10 thousand). When there is that substantial of a difference in the valuation of two companies, the company that is valued higher is likely to be a much better and more lucrative investment.

These are the various don'ts of penny stock trading that you must know to make a successful investment. If you follow the dos and avoid the don'ts of penny stock trading, and make sure you research and investigate any stock in which you are interested, penny stocks can be a great way to earn investment income.

# Chapter 10

# Penny Stock Myths

In this chapter, we will look at some of the myths that surround penny stocks and bust them.

## Penny stocks are not for beginners

No. This is just a myth. Penny stocks are for everyone. You don't have to be an expert trade in them. In fact, penny stocks are great for beginners, as it will expose them to how stock markets actually operate. It will show beginners how the stocks rise and fall within short periods of time and how that impacts their holdings, so beginners can very well start investing in penny stocks and start inviting substantial profits.

The trick to using penny stocks as an entry into the investment market is to start small. If you're spending a relatively low amount of money, the risk is lower because a loss will not have a significant impact on you. You can make mistakes and learn from them without depleting your savings or your investment budget, and every lesson will help you to make better choices about your penny stocks the next time around.

## Information on these stocks is highly elusive

No. This is just a misconception. It is understood that there is not much information available on penny stocks, but that does not mean you will not find any information on them. You have to look in all the right sources in order to land the right information. You can try asking your broker if he has any insider information. Having friends in the stock world can go a long way in helping you find the right kind of information. There are also websites that you can visit, but just make sure that the websites are independent of the companies that you are researching. There is information available, it just may be more difficult to find than information about other kinds of stocks.

## Penny stocks are complicated

Not necessarily. Penny stocks are not complicated, especially if you know how stocks in general operate. Penny stocks are regarded as easy topics to tackle, given how they can be quite predictable. If you brush up on the basics, you will surely be able to invest in them with ease.

The most complicated thing about penny stocks is getting the accurate information that you need to assess whether a penny stock is a good investment for you. Once you have that information, make sure you take all of the factors into consideration in your evaluation of the stock and of the company.

## Penny stocks should only be traded intraday

Not necessarily. Penny stocks can be held for long, as well, especially if you wish to command an incentive. You can profit from the difference in prices and also receive a dividend. The dividend might not be too big or substantial, but remaining invested in a few stocks will go a long way in helping you establish yourself in the stock market. Choosing stocks that earn dividends can also help to reduce the risk factor often associated with penny stocks, because even if the stock doesn't increase in value to any significant degree, you will still be earning some investment income.

## Penny stocks will not diversify your portfolio

Penny stocks will definitely diversify your portfolio. You do not have to always trade in them within a single day. Holding penny stocks can prove to be quite lucrative. You have to develop the intuition to know which stocks are worth holding and which need to be sold. Penny stocks can go a long way in helping you maintain a diverse portfolio.

## There is no scope for fraud in penny stocks

This is absolutely not true. There is ample scope for fraud in the world of penny stocks. There can be fraudulent companies that are simply floated for the sole purpose of conning people. You have to go through all the details of the company in order to know whether it is a genuine business or there is something fishy about it. You will also have to do the fundamental and technical analysis to be doubly sure about it.

A popular scam is for a company to use boiler room tactics to pressure investors into purchasing the stocks by strongly emphasizing the positives of a stock and ignoring or minimizing the negatives. If you are contacted about purchasing a penny stock by a broker using this kind of tactic, think twice about purchasing – there is a very good chance that you are not getting all of the necessary information about the company or the stock.

## Penny stocks will not garner large profits

This is just a myth. Penny stocks will surely help you garner large profits, given you pick the best ones. As you know, they are all mostly priced between $5 and under, but that does not mean they will not help you draw in large profits. In fact, their face value should have nothing to do with their potential. Suppose you bought 500 stocks priced at $4. In a year, the same ones are worth $15. You have obviously made a large profit through your investment. Also, penny stocks might help you draw in bigger profits as compared to regular stocks. It's a matter of remaining invested and showcasing patience.

## Shorting penny stocks won't cause much damage

This is not true. Just because they are penny stocks does not mean you can short them as and when you feel like. It is a golden rule to never short any stock unless absolutely necessary. If you short it unnecessarily then you will have to deal with a good investment going bad, unless you think the stocks in your possession are going to do extremely well in the future and you are confident about it.

## Penny stocks will never go wrong

This is not true at all. Just because they are cheap does not mean penny stocks will not go wrong. If you have bought stocks of a company that is not doing too well, your investment might go wrong. You have to do your research to ensure that you pick companies that are doing well and putting out substantial profits. Do your research first and don't follow advice blindly.

These are some myths that surround penny stocks, which will help you understand the topic better.

# Chapter 11

# Penny Stock FAQs

Here are some FAQs (frequently asked questions) on the topic of penny stocks that you need to understand in order to comprehend the topic better.

## Are penny stocks good investments?

Yes. Penny stocks are great investments. When it comes to stock market investments, there really is no universal yardstick to measure the value of one investment against another. You have to evaluate each one individually and not generalize about them. Penny stocks are great investment choices if you want something reliable and worthwhile to help you increase the value of your money. They can take in a small sum and cough up a big profit. The key is to understand what stocks to pick and what to avoid.

## Will penny stocks add to my existing portfolio?

Yes. Penny stocks will be a part of your existing portfolio. You can diversify your portfolio by investing in penny stocks and avail yourself of its benefits. Although they are priced low, they are still counted as bona fide stock market investments. Penny stocks are classified as company shares just like common or preferred stock. Regardless of how full your portfolio is, penny stocks will add a little "extra" to it and make it a bit more dependable in terms of positive output. So don't over-think the prospect of having penny stocks in your portfolio and add them in confidently.

## Should penny stocks be treated as risky investments?

Yes. Not just penny stocks but also all other stock market investments should be considered as risky. As you are well aware, the stock market can throw up both good and bad outcomes. Penny stocks do not enjoy any special privileges when it comes to that and you have to be prepared for anything that might come your way. Picking the right stocks will no doubt help you but there are no guarantees that it will always work that way. You should prepare for both profits and losses that might come your way.

## What is a good sum to invest in penny stocks?

That is entirely your choice to make. Many people start by investing a small sum to see how it goes for then and slowly build up on the value. If you think starting out with just $50 is a good idea for you, then you can consider it seriously. Given that most penny stocks remain within the $5 and $10 range, you don't have to worry about your budget going over-board and $50 can help you pull in a good amount of quality penny stocks. Once that pays off, you can invest in more.

## Can penny stocks be transferred?

Yes. Penny stocks can be transferred from one account to another if is mutual consent. Penny stocks are more or less regarded as regular stocks and you can transfer them from one account to another. You can speak with your trader or dealer to have them transferred. It might take a few days for the transaction to be processed and, once done, you will be able to see the details of the stocks in the transferee's account.

## Why are penny stocks sold OTC?

OTC or over-the-counter transactions are mostly carried out for all those investments that have small values attached to them. Such investments are not listed on any stock exchange and can only be purchased through a dealer network. Penny stocks, as you know, are valued between $5 and $10, which makes them ideal to be traded over the counter. This system is also known as pink sheets owing to the issuance of pink colored sheets that carry the bid and ask prices. Over the years, the system changed quite a bit and you might not see the same old pink sheets that were once used since mostly everything is now electronic.

## Should penny stocks be traded intraday?

Most people prefer to do so. Penny stocks have a lot of volatility and it is best for you to dispose of them within the same day. Doing so will help you prevent unnecessary risks that can plunge your investments into bad debts. That said, however, it might be best for you to hold on to some penny stocks for some time. It is highly subjective and you should make a call on it based on your assessment of the stocks.

Try trading in them on an intraday basis and once you get the hang of it, you can start holding your penny stocks.

## Is this book a thorough penny stock guide?

Yes. This book can be regarded as a thorough penny stock guide that will help you get started with penny stock trading. It will also allow you to make the right investment choices and improve the state of your investments. You can both diversify your portfolio and correct any past mistakes by investing in penny stocks.

## Can I short penny stocks?

Yes. Shorting is an option that is available for any investment in the stock market. Shorting refers to selling a stock that you don't own. You will have to borrow them from someone and then return it to them within a period of time. You, as the person indulging in the short, will wish that the penny stock's prices drop by the time you buy it back and return it. Shorting can pay off very well, provided you pick stocks that are doing well currently but will surely fall in value within a stipulated period of time. But there are risks involved here as well as the shorted stock's price might rise by the time you buy it back to return.

## What are some of the risks of penny stocks?

There are many risks involved in penny stocks. For starters, you have to be wary of their volatile prices. It can get extremely tough to predict your penny stock's price changes and it might go from high to low in no time at all. Second, penny stocks are not as easily available as regular stocks. You will have to wait a little before getting the stocks, as your dealer will have to find them for you.

These are the various FAQs on the topic to help you understand it better. Next we will take a look at some of the advantages and disadvantages of penny stock trading.

# Chapter 12

# Advantages and Disadvantages of Penny Stock Trading

Here are some prominent advantages and disadvantages of penny stocks that you can look into before deciding to take up trading. While we certainly think that the advantages outweigh the disadvantages by quite a lot, you will need to make up your own mind about whether it's the right thing for you or not.

## Advantages

Penny stocks are great investment choices for all those who wish to invest just a small amount in the stock market. If your budget is limited and you want to make the most of it, it is best for you to go with a penny stock. As you already know, these stocks are listed between $5 and $10, which makes them quite affordable even to a beginner. You can set yourself a fixed budget and use just the limited amount to start dealing in the stock market.

Penny stocks can pay off well if you know which ones to add to your portfolio of investments. Just by investing $100 to secure $3 shares and disposing of it at $5 at the end of the day, you can make a profit of $67, which is more than half of your initial investment. And this money comes to you within the course of a single day, which makes it ideal for all those who trade on a daily basis.

Some people use penny stocks as back-up investments in case something goes wrong with their regular investments. This means that they will have a few penny stocks traded on a daily basis and keep accumulating profits, which can offset some of the bad investments in their portfolio. In fact, you can turn to these stocks to help you out of debts that have come through your other investments.

## Disadvantages

You have to remember that volatility can act as a double-edged sword. On the one hand, it will help you lock in a big profit within a short amount of time; but, on the other hand, you might end up losing out on a large sum of money owing to the value of the stock dipping through the course of the day. Therefore, you have to learn to use volatility to allow you to buy more stocks when the prices are low and sell them when their value rises.

Liquidity is also a major problem when it comes to penny stocks. They are most definitely not as liquid as regular stocks because their demand and supply channels work unpredictably. What you think is a liquid stock might not be in keeping with how the rest of the market feels. This could leave you with a stock that is hard to dispose of and cause you to write that off as a bad debt. So the advice here is to pick stocks that are liquid and have precedent to support them. Look at any stock's history first before zeroing in on it.

You might find it a little difficult to find appropriate information on penny stocks. These stocks continue to be unpopular and tucked away from regular investors, so you have to dig deep in order to find stocks that are good investment choices for you. Your broker might not provide you with any substantial help when it comes to finding penny stocks and you have to get in touch with an agent who can buy and sell the stocks for you through the issuance of pink slips.

Penny stocks can be a bit tough to manipulate. If you are thinking of a scheme in which you raise a stock's popularity and then capitalize on it once it hits the upper circuit, you might have to put in a lot of effort. You will have to find people to influence and also support your claims with solid backing. All of this can turn very ambitious for something that is valued as low as $5.

# Chapter 13

# Important Terminologies to Understand

In closing, let's summarize some of the important terms that we have learned. Feel free to use this chapter as a glossary that you can use to easily look up terms in one place.

## Volatility

The word "volatility" often gets used in the stock market, yet not many know how to interpret it correctly. It refers to stock prices that move up and down rapidly owing to their elastic demand and supply. Penny stocks are extremely volatile owing to how often they are bought and sold. Thousands of these traders buy and sell these stocks within the course of a single day, thereby making them extremely volatile. But this is a quality that makes penny stocks ideal for those traders looking to make a quick buck. You don't have to wait months for your stock to rise or fall. Within the same day, you can remain with your profits. Volatility can sometimes be regarded as a great tool that penny stock enthusiasts can use to usher their investments into the right direction. However, you have to be extremely careful when it comes to handling extremely volatile stocks. Getting caught on the wrong end will crush both your investment and your spirit, so it is best that you first understand the general trend that the stock will follow before making your investment in it.

## Liquidity

Liquidity is another popular word in the stock market terminology that gets misinterpreted or is not understood at all. It refers to the ability to sell a stock in the market, which depends on how many people are willing to buy it. Say, for example, you have 10,000 shares of a company and there are 100 more investors with the same, making it a total of 1,000,000 shares floating in the market. There are only 5,000 buyers, making it extremely illiquid. You may not be able to dispose of your stocks even if you turn out to be the first one to queue it in the market. You will still be left with 5,000 unsold shares in your holding. This is a bit of a risk that you should be willing to take when dealing in penny stocks and the best way to avoid it is by taking a smaller position as opposed to a bigger one. Try to take many small penny stocks under your wing instead of one large portion of a single stock. Now let us look at what happens in a liquid market. Take the same example, where you are holding 10,000 shares and there are just five others with the same. That brings the total number of shares floating in the market to 50,000 shares. The demand for these shares is 100,000, meaning 100,000 people are willing to buy it at the price you have queued it up at. The shares will be easily disposed of and their value will considerably rise. It is best for you to buy stocks that are liquid as compared to illiquid stocks. You can avoid a lot of unnecessary debts by doing so and have the chance to dispose of all your penny stock holdings within the course of a single day.

## Share lockups

This is another term to ponder. Your shares can get locked up because an activity in the company represented by those shares. Say, for example, you have stocks of company A, which is going through an acquisition or merger. You will have to wait until as the deal is complete before being able to dispose of the stocks. Although most stocks do well after a merger or acquisition, the same cannot be said about IPO lockups. You might end up with a stock whose value plunges after the lockup is lifted.

## Market valuation

Also referred to as market capitalization (or market cap), this is a simple and straightforward way to determine the valuation of a company. You take the number of outstanding shares that a company has (i.e., the total number of shares issued), and multiply that by the stock price. For penny stocks, the market capitalization is usually in the range of $10 million to $100 million, which may sound like a lot but is quite low compared to many of the other types of stocks.

## Float

Float is the number of publicly owned shares that a company has available for trading. This does not include restricted shares (i.e., shares that are held by company insiders or bought privately) because those shares are not tradable and do not impact the trading stock unless the company issues too many, which can affect the company's overall valuation. "Low float" stocks, or stocks that have low numbers of publicly owned shares, tend to be more volatile because good news about the company can create a significant demand for the limited number of shares, causing the share price to spike drastically.

## Initial public offering (IPO)

The IPO process occurs when a previously private company makes its first issue of stock available for sale to the public. The capital from this first sale usually goes to the company, although company insiders may profit to some degree, as well.

Going through the IPO process is how a company gets to be listed on a stock exchange. The process is quite lengthy and complicated and involves meeting with SEC officials, banks, and other relevant parties to determine whether the company meets the necessary minimum requirements and what the company's value should be. It is rare for a penny stock company to go through the IPO process because most would not meet the minimum requirements.

## Merger

A merger occurs when two companies join together and combine stocks. The purpose is usually to reduce costs by having the combined entity be more efficient. Generally speaking, when a merger of two companies is announced, one of the company's share prices will rise, and the other will drop. The analysis surrounding share price valuation as impacted by mergers is extremely complicated and is usually only carried out by high-level traders with significant resources. If you are dealing in penny stocks, mergers will not likely impact the stocks that you are trading in. Also, it is recommended that you ignore potential merger investments because there is only a small chance that you will be more likely than the big-time investors to make the correct choices and take advantage of the merger in a way that will earn you profit.

Unlike mergers, reverse mergers are more likely to have an impact on penny stocks. A reverse merger is a relatively cheap and fast way to lower a company's value to initiate an

IPO, so it is an approach often taken by penny stock companies and by developmental companies. Reverse mergers can be a positive thing for a penny stock investor because it makes more stock available to trade and can be a great way to cheaply get in on the ground floor of a developmental company while it is still at the penny stock stage of its growth.

## Share lockup

A share lockup is a period of time when the shares of a company are restricted from trading. This often happens after a merger, an IPO, or some kind of acquisition. Lockups resulting from an IPO usually range from six months to a year, while lockups from other types of transactions can be as long as a few years. If you know ahead of a time that a lockup will occur, this can be a good time to get some deals because a lot of investors will be looking to sell their shares before they are unable to do so for a lengthy period. This can cause the stock prices to fall. If you choose the right stocks, once the lockup period is over, the stock price will likely rise, and you can make a good profit.

## Dilution

This is the decrease in proportional ownership of a company when the company issues additional shares. For example, if you hold 100,000 shares in Company A, and Company A has a total of 1 million outstanding shares, you own 10% of Company A. If the shares are valued at $5 each, your investment is worth $500,000. If Company A issues another 500,000 shares in order to raise funds for a project, you now own only 6.7% of Company A. Dilution may be worth it if it ends up making the company more profitable overall, but you will want to keep an eye on why the dilution occurred and what effect it is having both on your investment and on the company.

## Upside

The upside is the forecasted percentage increase or dollar amount increase in a stock's price. The higher a stock's upside, the more potential value a stock has. It essentially means that a stock's true value is higher than the current stock price reflects. Investment analysis uses two different methods to determine a stock's upside: technical analysis or fundamental analysis.

Technical analysis looks at the stock's price on a historical basis to determine any patterns. A breakout from the stock's price trend will increase the stock's upside potential. For example, if a stock has consistently traded between $1 and $5 per share, and suddenly the price rises to $10, this is a breakout and would indicate that the stock price's upside potential is over $10. A stock in this situation would be a good investment to pursue.

A fundamental analysis is the process of assessing the financial fundamentals of the company in order to determine the company's ability to generate earnings and sales. A company that is able to manage its costs well and increase profit margins will be considered to have a higher upside.

Evaluating whether a stock has upside potential is a critical part of assessing whether you should invest in that stock. If the stock seems to be more of a fad than a substantial stock for a company that has good financial fundamentals, the best choice would be to move on and look for a different penny stock to invest in.

## Resistance and Support

Resistance refers to the situation where a stock's price has increased and has eventually settled at a point where many investors decide that they want to sell. This will usually prevent the stock price from rising further, at least for a while, because the stock is available to purchasers at that price so there is not battling for the stock that would usually cause a price increase.

Support is the opposite of resistance; it is where the stock price has been consistently decreasing and reaches a point where the shareholders want to sell.

## Breakouts and Breakdowns

When a stock's price somehow manages to break through a period of resistance and increase above the resistance point, this is called a breakout. Conversely, if a stock's price moves below the support point, it is called a breakdown. If this occurs, the stock would be considered very bearish; if you own such stock, you will need to consider whether you should sell it at that point, or if a significant enough loss has already occurred that you might as well hold on to the stock and hope that its value rises again sometime in the future.

## Market orders, limit orders, and stop loss orders

A market order is a sell, buy, or short order that is made at whatever the current market price is. This means that you agree to buy, sell, or short the order at the current market price, regardless of what that price ends up being. Market orders can be quite risky, as you can incur a significant loss if you are not paying attention to the most up-to-date market price. By avoiding market orders, you could potentially miss out on a great investment if, for instance, the current market price sank drastically as you were buying, or the current market price rose quickly as you were selling. These situations are rare, and it is much more likely that you will incur a loss.

A limit order is basically the opposite of a market order, in that you specify exactly what price you are willing to pay (or take, if you are selling). The trade will only go through if the person on the other side of the transaction agrees with your limit price. Limit orders are much less risky than market orders because you know exactly what you will be paying or earning.

Stop loss orders are orders that you place to liquidate your stock when a price that you have specified (as set out in the rules of investment that you set for yourself) has been reached or surpassed. A stop loss order will allow you to prevent large losses or protect your gains, depending on the situation. A stop loss order basically reflects the limits that you have set for yourself when it comes to how much you are willing to lose or spend.

A trailing stop loss order is set at a percentage below the current market price, whatever that market price may be so that it fluctuates with the market price of the stock. This allows you to protect your losses while still following your investment plan and the rules that you have set yourself about how much loss you will accept.

These are the important terminologies that you should know while dealing in penny stocks.

# Chapter 14

# Exchanges, Market Traders and Market Indices

## Exchanges

There are many types of market exchanges, as described below.

- Pink sheets

The pink sheets market is where a group of agents deal in penny stocks that are pretty tiny in value. They will mostly be under $5 and will not be listed on a stock exchange. If you think they will prove to be good investment choices, you can consider them, but remember that they will come with their own disadvantages. Many old hands prefer to not invest in these types of stocks owing to their illiquidity.

- Over-the-counter bulletin boards

As is the case with pink sheets, OTCBB are also traded over the counter. Here, too, the stocks traded are less than $5. But these are slightly more reliable as compared to the ones traded in the pink sheets market. OTCBB stocks can be bought and sold conveniently once you get in touch with the dealer circuit.

- NASDAQ small market

NASDAQ is an online market place where stocks are bought and sold electronically. You need not rely on "on-the-floor" brokers and can buy and sell your stocks by yourself. The regular NASDAQ lists regular stocks and does not entertain penny stocks. But the NASDAQ small market almost exclusively caters to penny stocks, making it easy for you to find and buy them.

- NASDAQ national market

The NASDAQ national market involves only electronic trading and is done mostly on technology-related stocks. It involves almost exclusively high-priced stocks so, if you are dealing only in penny stocks, you will not be participating in the NASDAQ national market.

- Amex

Amex is possibly the most popular stock exchange in America. At the American stock exchange, you will find all those stocks that are really tiny and range between $3 and $5. Although the pricing looks great here, you might have to wait a long time before seeing any substantial profits. Therefore, it is best for you to avoid investing in any stocks that lie within this small range.

- NYSE

The NYSE is the oldest and biggest stock exchange in the world. However, you will not find any penny stocks here, as it does not encourage those that are priced too low or move too slow. So this market will not provide a base for penny stock investors.

These are the various markets that you have to acquaint yourself with in order to start dealing in penny stocks.

**Market traders**

Market traders are all those who are trading in the stock market. As you know, there will be a variety of traders in the market, all of whom have different backgrounds. Here are some of them.

- Amateurs

Amateurs are those who are just starting out in the stock market. These amateurs will repeatedly make the same mistakes over and over again. They prove to be easy targets, whom you can easily target and draw money from. If you think you are an amateur trader who is making unnecessary mistakes, it is best for you to improve the situation by stopping all your trading and coming up with a better trading plan to follow.

- Independent trader

Independent traders are those who use their very own capital to deal in stocks. If you wish to be one, you have to start out with a capital sum that is entirely yours and invest it in the market. Independent traders can also be seen as sole proprietors, as any liability that will come through their investments shall entirely be borne by the individual investor alone. A majority of the investors in the penny stock market fall into this category.

- Market makers

Market makers are those people who influence the market by pumping into certain stocks and raising their popularity. Once its popularity rises, many people invest in the stock. This makes it great for the investor, as he or she will be able to capitalize upon its success. They will, however, decide to withdraw from the stocks without warning and forget about the others that helped them in raising the value of the stocks.

- Institutional traders

These are people who are employed by companies to trade for them. They mostly do not venture into penny stocks owing to their volatility. They will trade almost entirely in big stocks that are doing well. Institutional traders are mostly interested in building up their portfolios to increase their values exponentially investment after investment.

These are the various types of traders in the stock market.

**Market indices**

Market indices are market averages. All stock markets have an average that is calculated based on the total number of shares doing the rounds and the varying prices. Here are some market indices to look into.

- The Wilshire 500 is a big index; almost all stocks that are traded in the NYSE, Amex, NASDAQ, and other exchanges will be taken into consideration here. Although some penny stocks are considered, there are not too many of them. So this might not be the right index for you to look at when you are dealing in penny stocks.

- The next index is the Russell 2000. The Russell 2000 is great for penny stock traders, as it lists several small company stocks that are traded publically. Here, stocks listed in the NASDAQ small cap, pink sheets, and OTCBB will be listed, so you will have a clear idea of the general directions that the stocks in particular categories are following and which ones you can invest with.

- Dow Jones 30 is the next market index to consider. This index uses 30 of the most popular companies to generate an average. And it is no surprise that these 30 do not include any penny stock companies. So don't expect to use this index while dealing in these stocks.

- The S&P 500 is the biggest index in the American stock exchange. It takes into consideration 500 of the most widely invested stocks in the market. However, these 500 include not a single penny stock company, thereby making this index completely useless for penny stock investors. You can look beyond it when you wish to invest in these stocks.

These are the different indexes to consider in the stock market. As you can see, the ones that cater to penny stocks are quite low in number as opposed to those meant for regular stocks.

*James Hawk*

# Chapter 15

# Types of Brokers and Promoters

## Brokers

Brokers are important parts of the stock market whom you might have to consider in order to make the right investment choices.

Brokers don't necessarily have to be advisors only; they can play many roles. Regardless of the type of broker that you choose to work with, there are six important factors to take into consideration about brokers in general before you sign up with one:

1) They have to be licensed. This involves passing two exams issued by the Financial Industry Regulatory Authority, Inc. (FINRA). If passed, the exams

demonstrate that the broker has knowledge about trading and about the legal aspects that govern the securities industry. If a broker does not have these credentials, do not think twice: run far and run fast.

2) They have to make money. There are various fee structures that brokers will use, but all of them need to get paid – it is their job, after all. The important thing is to review the fee structure that they offer and be clear about any and all potential costs. You need to choose the broker and the fee structure that suits you.

3) They are not always good people. Brokers have access to a lot of information about securities that is not available to the general public. Sometimes they take advantage of this information. They are not all bad, but some definitely are. Keep an ear to the ground for anything that you can find on a broker's reputation. See if you can get recommendations from other investors whom you trust. Always pay attention to how your stocks are doing with your broker so that you can continuously assess whether your broker is helping you or taking advantage of you.

4) They often have hidden fees. As discussed under the "they have to make money" section, you need to be aware of any and all costs that might be associated with your broker's services. Ask the necessary questions to make sure that you know about any potential costs. Also, be aware of any minimum account requirements. Even if you start off above the minimum, you could potentially go below that, and there could be costs associated with that. Always read the fine print before you sign up with a broker.

5) There are a lot of different kinds of brokers. This section will go through the different kinds, and will give you information that will help you to decide which type of broker will work best for you. Remember that price is not the only factor that you need to consider. The types of services that are offered and the level of support that the broker provides are two more important factors that you should consider before you make your decision as to which type of broker and which specific broker you will sign on with.

6) They are restricted by the pattern day trader (PDT) rule. The SEC has a rule that any investor with less than $25,000 in their brokerage account is limited to three round-trip trades (i.e., buying and selling stock on the same day) per week. While you may wish to do more than that, remember that if a broker is willing to bend or break the law for that matter, they are probably not trustworthy in other areas. It is better to find legal ways to work around the restriction than to try and get your broker to ignore the rule.

- Regular brokers

Regular brokers are those who have the job of buying and selling stocks for you. That pretty much sums up their job requirement and they do not venture into suggesting any stocks to you or anyone. These are also known as part-time brokers and will be required to do as you say. Hiring these will help you get started with the stock market on the right foot. Regular brokers don't necessarily have to be tied to a financial firm and you can independently employ them. They will charge you just a small sum for their service and you don't have to set a big budget to afford one. However, some of these brokers can be paid by their firm to mislead you. Even if it is not part of their job to advise you on the stocks to pick, they will purposely suggest some bad ones to throw you off. That is where you have to be a bit careful with them. Do your research before employing a regular broker and check his or her credentials first.

- Full-time brokers

Full-time brokers are those whose job it is to take care of your investments full time. They are specialized brokers who have extensive knowledge of the stock markets and when, where, and how much to invest. Full-time brokers can be quite expensive because of the amount of work that they provide. It entails going beyond buying and selling the stocks and involves doing due research on the best stocks to buy. Here, your full-time broker may or may not be interested in trading penny stocks for you. They will mostly like to trade only in big company stocks that are a bit predictable. Therefore, these might not be good brokers for you to choose to carry out your stock market transactions. However, you can consider them if penny stocks are not going to be your only investment choice.

- Boiler-room brokers

Boiler-room brokers are those that are planted to mislead the public. They are people that you should be wary of and avoid engaging with. Their main job is to draw in suckers and cheat them. They will go to any length to do so. They will know all the tricks of the trade to influence a particular stock and end up causing the investors huge losses. Boiler-room brokers are therefore some of the dreaded. It might be tough to spot one though as they will be well disguised. They will act as if they are genuinely interested in providing you with quality advice but that will not be a part of their actual agenda.

- Online traders

Online traders are those who work through online sites to buy and sell your stocks. They can be independent or tied to a firm. You can ask them for advice as well and also to have your stocks traded. Online traders prefer to trade in stocks that are predictable, as compared to taking risks. They can charge you a little more than your regular brokers, as they will have quite a bit of expertise. If you are an amateur and looking for a good broker to get you started, these are the ones you have to approach. Then again, you have to ensure that these aren't boiler-room brokers that are out to cheat you.

- Floor brokers

Floor brokers are those who operate from the floor of the stock exchange. They work in the stock exchange and take in orders to execute. These are slightly hard to pin down, especially if you wish to get them to trade in penny stocks, so they are not the ones that you should be considering.

These are the various types of brokers that you have to consider to carry out your stock market transactions for you.

- Promoters

Many of the promoters in the investment industry are looking to trick unsuspecting and amateur investors into making foolish investment decisions that will benefit only the promoter and the company that been hired them. While they are often not trustworthy, watching their patterns can provide you with indications about market trends that may guide you in the right direction in terms of investments.

- Penny stock pickers

Penny stock pickers are promoters who focus only or primarily on penny stocks, due to the penny stock's tendency to be highly volatile and the lack of information necessary to make an educated investment decision. Penny stock pickers will often make promises about how much a penny stock's price is expected to increase. Do not take these promises seriously; these pickers have no way of knowing that the price will rise that much, and they are just saying it to take advantage of your investment excitement.

- Guru stock pickers

Unlike penny stock pickers, guru stock pickers actually do an extensive amount of research into the market before they choose which stocks to promote. Unfortunately, this means that they rarely deal with penny stocks because the fundamentals of penny stocks are not usually available to assist them in making a proper analysis. Guru stock pickers tend to focus on bigger companies, particularly those listed on the major exchanges that have minimum reporting requirements.

- TV, print, and online advertisers

While commentators in the media may provide a lot of information about companies on the market exchanges, they are legally prevented from addressing penny stocks. It is best not to look to these commentators for assistance or guidance on penny stocks because the information will not be there.

- Newsletters

Newsletters are invariably produced by marketing companies hired by penny stock companies or their shareholders to distribute "research" about the companies. The newsletter creators are legally obligated to disclose if they have been paid to make recommendations, but even if they have not been paid directly, they are rarely completely without bias. You should not take recommendations from them directly, but they can offer a useful indication of market trends in general.

- Analysts

Analysts are professionals who are usually trained or educated in the area of trading. The problem with analysts is that, like gurus, they tend to focus only on the stocks that are traded on the major exchanges. If you see an analyst making a recommendation on a penny stock, make sure you do some research into that analyst's background and qualifications before deciding if you will take the recommendation.

- Economists

Similar to analysts, economists are trained and educated in the area of finance and economics. Again, just like analysts, they tend to focus almost exclusively on companies that are traded on the major stock exchanges, so they are of little help if you are dealing only with penny stocks.

Options penny stocks

There can be many types of stock market investments. Not everything will be the same and some investment types will not correspond to the traditional way of trading.

One such unconventional method of trading is known as "options."

Options are regarded as among the most versatile forms of investment in the stock markets. These options more or less favor the seller owing to their predictability. Options are good choices to invest with if you plan on venturing into something unique while leaving behind the standard.

Options trading is also regarded by many as a risky form of trading because of the high level of risk. However, in all fairness, risk is a part and parcel of pretty much any form of investment avenue and does not pertain to options alone. Therefore, you need not worry about options being "riskier" than the other forms of investments and can confidently invest in them without worrying too much about the outcome.

That being said, you will have to go through what the particular options can do for you in terms of output and only then invest in them. Not all options will help you earn a big profit and there will always be some that will cause you a loss.

Before you do that, you have to understand what these options are. Here is an example for you to understand how it works.

Suppose I asked you to buy a fancy watch for $100. After checking the watch, you agree and offer to pay me $50 towards reserving the watch. I agree to do so and reserve it for you on the condition that you will pay me the rest of the money within the next two weeks.

During the next two weeks, you find out that the watch belonged to Brad Pitt and is worth $500. You immediately decide to settle the deal with me and claim the watch by paying the $50. I cannot demand a higher value for the watch anymore, since I have already agreed to sell it for exactly $100.

On the other hand, an alternate situation might crop up during the two weeks. You might find out that the watch is actually a duplicate and is worth $20. In that case, you can refuse to buy the watch from me citing its worthlessness and forfeit the deal. However, you will have to forgo the $50 that you paid towards the watch as advance money.

This chance that you take to refuse honoring the deal is known as an "option."

Let us now look at a real stock market example.

Suppose a trader has in his possession 100 penny stocks of a company that he is offering at $8 each. The buyer agrees to purchase the stocks at that price and pays an advance of

$200. The trader agrees to it and reserves the stocks on the condition that the buyer pays for them within the next 1 week.

During the week, the buyer finds out that the stock is actually great and is being undervalued. The real value of the stock is $10, which means the seller will make a $2 profit per share. He decides to immediately settle the deal in order to capitalize on the stock. The seller will make an overall profit of $200. This is great, considering penny stocks are generally low-priced and the trader capitalized on it within a short period of time.

Alternately, the trader finds out that the stock is actually overvalued and its actual current market value is $5. This means that the buyer will have to lose $3 per share should he choose to honor the deal. At this point, the smart choice is for the buyer to refuse taking up the deal. Although he will be losing out on the $200 paid as advance, it will still be better than taking a bigger loss on the deal.

Penny stock options can be a little hard to come because of traders' lack of interest in investing in stocks that are volatile. However, looking for it in all the right places can help you find some that will help you add to your portfolio positively.

<u>Types</u>

There are two types of options to choose from, American and European. American options are the most common type. They are quite flexible in that you can decide to settle them any time before the maturity date of the option.

European options, on the other hand, do not provide flexibility. They have to be settled at the time of maturity alone and not any time before. This makes them less preferred as compared to American options.

These are just names that are given to the stocks and have nothing to do with the geographical aspect.

Remember that penny stocks aren't the only securities that options apply to. They can have many other forms of underlying financial securities as well.

<u>Advantages</u>

There are many advantages to dealing in options. For starters, you have the opportunity to refuse a deal if you think it is not going your way. You will be able to avoid a bad debt by refusing to honor the deal. Another advantage is that you don't have to pay the entire amount upfront and can do so in installments. Many people prefer options owing to their high payoff rate. You can easily capitalize on a good stock within a short period of time and not worry about having to wait long for it.

Disadvantages

The main disadvantage of options is that you have to be careful in picking out the best ones to deal in. if you don't have any relevant experience with them, it is best for you to avoid venturing into them without doing proper research. Try to understand everything that goes into successfully trading options before making your move. Options can also be a little volatile in that, you might have equal chances of earning a profit or suffering a loss. Although it's been mentioned that you can quickly turn around a profit, it might not always be possible for you to do so and will only happen if you have an eye for picking stocks that are genuinely great to invest with.

Although options come with a fair share of ups and downs, you have to consider it as a good investment option.

# Chapter 16

# Important Penny Stock Rules to Swear By

Here are some penny stock golden rules to swear by. If you take nothing else away from the book, these are the fundamental ideas that should stick with you. Hopefully you will go far using these.

The penny stock market is extremely volatile and there will be very little to no margin for error. Therefore, you have to be extremely careful with it and make sure that you take all the necessary precautions to safeguard your investments, well in advance. Make it a point to have a buffer in place that will prevent your investments from crashing. This can be through the implementation of a stop loss strategy or by setting a limit within which to trade.

If you think you have made a bad investment choice, you must indulge in damage control as soon as possible. Don't think it will fix itself with time, as you have to be pretty proactive in the penny stock market to avoid suffering heavy losses. You have to stave off giving into your ego and correct whatever mistake you have already made. Go through the details of your transactions to pick out the mistakes and fix them as soon as you can to prevent any further damage. You should learn a lesson or two and not repeat the same mistakes again.

When you think of investing in penny stocks, you should think of it as a full-time hobby. You cannot invest in one and forget about it. You should make it a point to keep a close watch on your stocks. Observe their trends and see how the stocks are faring. If they are doing well, continue to keep an eye on them; as soon as one reaches the ideal point, you can quickly dispose of it. On the other hand, if one is not doing too well, dispose it without batting an eyelid. It is better to dispose of a bad stock than to wait for it to pick up pace, the chances of which can be pretty low.

You have to reconstitute your priority list when it comes to trading in penny stocks. It is important to note that the smaller gains are much more valuable than the bigger ones, which actually are hard to come by, so your main goal should be to aim at the smaller profits that you can make and not obsess over any big opportunities that you missed out on. You have to be quick and invest in prospective stocks that will do well within a short period.

One great strategy to adopt in the penny stock market is shorting your stocks. Shorting, as you know, refers to borrowing stocks, selling them and then buying them back to return. Doing so helps you derive a great profit. Given how volatile the penny stock market is, you have to carefully pick a few stable stocks if you wish to remain with good profit and be able to capitalize on your strategy.

You have to be ready to take calculated risks. Calculated risks are those where you know exactly the amount that you will lose should your investment go wrong, so you have to be ready with a sum in mind that you are willing to lose without complaining. This sum should always be much lower than the profit that you wish to attain from the same investment. Say, for example, you wish to attain a profit of $50 with an $80 investment and the risk you are willing to take here is $20. This is a very rough example and you should indulge in a more calculated one where you know exactly how much money is going in and how much will be gained or lost once the investment goes through.

Do not make the mistake of copying someone else's strategies when it comes to stock investments. You have to come up with your very own strategy that will work well for you. You can work closely with an advisor or broker who will help you come up with a plan. On the other hand, it is best to keep your trading strategy a secret if you wish to keep your winning streak going. Sharing knowledge can be acceptable but not giving away your trade secrets.

Don't be too stuck on any one strategy to deal in penny stocks. You have to consider both long- and short-term strategies when it comes to investing in these stocks. Try to hold on to the stocks that are doing well so that you can capitalize on their long-term gains and sell the ones that lie on a regressive curve.

Don't start trading in the penny stock market by having a biased opinion about it. You should look at it as any other potential investment avenue and not necessarily one where you might run into greater risk. Risk is a part and parcel of any investment venture and you have to consider it a part of your trading strategy.

One golden rule to swear by is to never lose track of your investments. Don't make the mistake of not knowing where your money lies and how it is being used in the market. You have to keep track of all your money — pie to pie — and ensure that you know exactly how much is invested in the market.

It is pure gold to find an undervalued penny stock. Undervalued stocks are those that are priced too low. Once people realize their true value, they will scamper to buy these stocks, so you have to get there first in order to capitalize on the situation. You can easily derive huge profits just by investing in such stocks at the right time.

As you know, there will also be over-valued stocks in the market that you have to avoid. If you are not aware of how to do the calculations, you can consider seeking an expert who will help you out. He or she can provide you with the right information in terms of the stocks' valuation.

Remember: no risk, no gain. You have to be prepared to take a risk in order to attain a big enough profit. Don't refrain from taking a chance with an unpredictable stock. You will have the chance to learn from the experience. You can also consider setting aside a certain sum that will exclusively be invested in risky stocks.

Penny stocks should be a part of your portfolio, but not your entire portfolio. You should invest just a small sum in them, not a hefty one. Plan a budget well in advance instead of simply going with the flow. You should consider setting a limit that should not be crossed in a month. You can also consider setting a profit margin, after reaching which you will not trade in penny stocks for the rest of the month.

Be wary of any newsletters that you receive from online portals. These are known to purposely spread wrong messages and suggest bad stocks. You have to do thorough research on the topic before making any investments.

Don't panic when a stock goes down. You have to invest faith in it and wait for the stock to pick up pace once again. Even if it does go down, you have to understand that that is exactly how the stock market operates. The value of stocks keeps going up and down and you have to remain ready for any situation that comes your way. If you have done due research and know for sure that the company will not let you down, you have nothing to worry about.

*James Hawk*

# Key Highlights

Penny stocks are those that are generally priced at $5 or less. Although extremely rare these days, there was a time when penny stocks were valued at a penny or less, hence the name. Penny stocks are generally bought and sold over the counter, as they are not listed in regular stock markets. But that does not make them any less of a choice for lucrative investments. You have to view them on the same plane as you would regular stocks and think of them as great investment vessels. Penny stocks are sometimes also referred to as cent stocks in countries outside of the US.

There are many concepts, unique to penny stocks, which you must understand in detail before making any investments. These concepts will help you make the right decisions for your stocks and prevent you from making a mistake.

Penny stocks can be extremely powerful financial securities, given their high rate of volatility. They experience a lot of ups and downs within the same day, which makes them ideal for creating profits. But don't be under the impression that they will help you reel in millions overnight. That only happens in movies. You have to remain patient with your investments and only then will you see substantial profits coming your way.

Day trading is a trend that has gained popularity owing to its practical benefits. Day trading can help you earn daily profits that will be much higher than you would make if you held on to the stocks.

Profit and loss are part of stock market investments. You cannot always remain with a profit or a loss and must strike a fine balance between the two. Only highly experienced investors will be able to cut down on losses and capitalize on good stocks that will give them high-level profits.

You have to craft yourself an exclusive watch list that contains all the stocks that you wish to keep an eye on. Doing so will give you instant access to all the stocks that you have invested in, so you know whether they are doing well or not. You can create multiple watch lists if you like and differentiate them based on their categories.

Once you get the hang of it, you will find it easy to predict the trends that penny stocks will follow. You will have the chance to invest in one that will allow you to remain invested for a long time and also help you capitalize on its volatility. You have to learn to embrace the fact that penny stock prices fluctuate so much. With time, you will see that these very fluctuations are what are helping you bring in your profits.

You must avoid assessing stocks superficially and delve into their depths to understand properly how they function. You must perform both fundamental and technical analysis to know if a stock will do well or not. Some stocks will surge out of the blue, while some others will plummet. It is up to you to predict them correctly and ensure you do right by them.

You can use the prediction methods mentioned earlier to understand what it takes to predict the trend that a penny stock will follow. If you are able to successfully predict, it will make it easier for you to avoid making bad investments.

We looked at some myths that surround penny stocks that you must know in order to understand the topic in a better way.

You have to diversify your portfolio as much as possible to cut down on risks. Diversification means building a portfolio that contains penny stocks belonging to different categories. When you have that, you automatically reduce the risks and heighten your chances of ringing in profits.

Patience is extremely important in the stock market. You have to remain invested for a while before seeing sizeable profits. Don't be tempted to sell a good stock just because someone else is selling it. They might be getting the timing wrong and waiting it out might help you derive a bigger profit.

In order to get started with your penny stocks, you should set yourself up first. This includes setting up the computer system, finding a reliable connection, finding a financial firm, a broker, etc. All of these need to be done in a sequence in order to get started on the right foot.

Penny stock options are great for all those who wish to have a little more control and flexibility with their investments. Options mean buying a stock in installments, so you first pay only a small amount to reserve it and then settle it in full. At the same time, you can refuse paying it in full and decide to forfeit the deal. Options are also easier to work with than buying and selling regular stocks.

You have to familiarize yourself with some of the terms that are generally used in the stock market in order to experience smooth transactions. Your broker will not be interested in breaking it down for you and explaining everything in detail. You have to make the effort to know the words and their meanings. You can read through the terminologies again to acquaint yourself better.

We looked at the different advantages and disadvantages of penny stocks. Any financial security will come with its fair share of ups and downs and you have to prepare for both profits and losses. Just waiting for the profits and ignoring the potential losses can cause you to lose money. If you forget to keep track of your investments, assuming they are doing well, you might be surprised at what awaits you.

Penny stock investments should be treated as a full-time hobby and not taken casually.

You should acquaint yourself with the different types of brokers. These brokers are all meant to serve different purposes and you should pick the one that will do well for you. It is important for you to choose the right broker for yourself, depending on what type of investments you wish to make in the stock market. One great criterion to look into while choosing the right broker is the fees that they will charge. If you think they are charging you too much, it is best for you to look at another one. When you hit upon the right broker, you have to make efforts to establish proper communication in order to avoid unwanted misunderstanding.

You can consider picking a penny stock mentor who will guide you through the market. The mentor should be someone who has vast experience in trading penny stocks and will be able to guide you properly. If you wish to, you may also consult penny-picking sites that will suggest the best penny stocks to buy. But be careful, not all these sites are reliable and you have to do some much-required research before opting to pump your money into buying certain stocks. Even if the stocks are valued low, you will run the risk of undertaking a loss if the company is a bad one.

*James Hawk*

# Conclusion

I thank you once again for choosing this book and I hope you had a good time reading it.

The main aim of this book was to educate you on the basic concepts of penny stocks, which will help you get started on the right foot, and to provide you with a thorough explanation of the more in-depth and complicated aspects of penny stock trading.

We explored the definitions of the basic concepts of penny stock trading and some more complex ideas and terminologies. We examined the ways in which penny stock prices are determined and evaluated, which factors will impact the share price, and how to carry out an analysis of a company's share price in order to determine which stock is a good investment for you.

We also looked at general and more specific rules and guidelines that you are advised to follow in order to avoid significant losses and hopefully earn a good profit on your investments.

We talked about the different sources of information that will be available to you, including the various kinds of people whom you will likely encounter during your time in the penny stock trading world. We also discussed when you should trust these people and sources and when you should avoid them.

There are many people in the trading industry who are looking to profit off of you. Some of them will do so while also helping you and others will not be concerned about whether or not you make good investment decisions. Knowing who to trust and who to avoid can play a significant role in your investment success.

Now that you have finished reading this book, you have all of the information necessary to start your endeavor into penny stock trading and begin choosing which penny stocks you will purchase.

Penny stocks, as a concept, are not tough to understand and you can start investing in them once you comprehend the basics. Remember to consistently keep yourself educated about the market. A subscription to *Forbes* or other great trading magazines or newspapers can be of great help, as well.

You can go through this book again if you'd like to know exactly what it takes to invest in the right stocks. Reviewing the key highlights section will remind you of some of the essential aspects of penny stock trading, if you are looking for a quick refresher. Do not hesitate to go back over any section of the book if you feel that you are not clear on a concept, or if you need to revisit an idea to make sure that you are making educated and informed investment decisions.

Once you feel that you are ready, take the leap and start purchasing stocks! We know that the trading world can sometimes seem overwhelming and complicated, but this book has armed you with all of the information that you require to be able to make decisions that will lead you toward profit and away from losses.

Remember to do your research, and always get as much information as you can about a company and its stocks before you decide to invest. A thorough assessment of all available information can make the difference between earning a substantial profit, and incurring a substantial loss.

Once you start investing, you will have to keep track of your expenses to ensure that you are spending within your limit and not going overboard. Always keep in mind your investment plan and your rules for investment, as we discussed in this book. If you stick to these guidelines, you will avoid making a snap or emotional investment decision that you will likely regret down the line.

Remember your goals, and focus on them if you are ever feeling frustrated with your investments and how long it may take to earn a profit. As we have said, there will be times when you will feel discouraged, but this is a normal and common part of trading and investing. It is very rare for everything to go an investor's way. Everyone makes mistakes, but as long as you learn from those mistakes, you will gradually increase your investment earnings.

I wish you luck with your penny stock endeavors and hope you find success.

Best of luck!

*James Hawk*

Made in the USA
Middletown, DE
12 March 2020

86264198R00108